**Secure
Our
Ship!
Fuel
America
Now!**

**Supercharge America's Economy
and End Global Warming
by Developing ALL
America's Energy Resources!**

# COUNTER-INTUITIVE?

Unless America develops all available energy resources, Americans cannot create the strong economy essential for funding the development and implementation of technology to monitor and control atmospheric $CO_2$; permanently ending global warming!

Author: E. Roman Hawley
Copyright: 2013, E. Roman Hawley

Copyright © 2013 by E. Roman Hawley
All rights reserved. This book or any portion thereof
may not be reproduced or used in any manner whatsoever
without the express written permission of the publisher
except for the use of brief quotations in a book review.

Printed in the United States of America
First Printing, 2013

ISBN: 0991212304
ISBN 13: 9780991212309

**BizzEB.com, LLC** (Pronounced: Bizz-E-B)
817 Krueger Pkwy
Stuart, FL 34996

# DEDICATION.

## William (Bill) Stroman

Without Bill assuming the responsibility of the business,
moving me 'out to pasture';
this book would not have been possible!

# CONTENTS

1 Important Definitions · · · · · · · · · · · · · · · · · · · · · vii
2 Introduction · · · · · · · · · · · · · · · · · · · · · · · · · · · · 1
3 America, Energy, Environment & Politics · · · · · · · · · · 7
4 Why Is Energy So Important? · · · · · · · · · · · · · · · · · 13
5 Carbon Based Life and CO2 · · · · · · · · · · · · · · · · · · 17
6 Global Warming Data, Statistics & Research · · · · · · · · 20
7 Is there a CO2 and Global Warming
  Cause and Effect Relationship? · · · · · · · · · · · · · · · · 23
8 What Can America Do About Global Warming? · · · · · · 33
9 America's Energy Options · · · · · · · · · · · · · · · · · · · 40
10 Energy Markets and Trading · · · · · · · · · · · · · · · · · 42
11 Oil, More than Just Energy · · · · · · · · · · · · · · · · · · 48
12 The Long Term Impact of Refinery Exports? · · · · · · · · 51
13 Conventional Oil · · · · · · · · · · · · · · · · · · · · · · · · 53
14 Shale Oil · · · · · · · · · · · · · · · · · · · · · · · · · · · · · 59
15 Oil Shale · · · · · · · · · · · · · · · · · · · · · · · · · · · · · 62
16 CO₂ Oil · · · · · · · · · · · · · · · · · · · · · · · · · · · · · · 68
17 Coal · · · · · · · · · · · · · · · · · · · · · · · · · · · · · · · · 72
18 Natural Gas · · · · · · · · · · · · · · · · · · · · · · · · · · · 75
19 Nuclear Power · · · · · · · · · · · · · · · · · · · · · · · · · 77
20 Biofuels · · · · · · · · · · · · · · · · · · · · · · · · · · · · · 80
21 Hydro-Power · · · · · · · · · · · · · · · · · · · · · · · · · · 84
22 Geo-Thermal Power · · · · · · · · · · · · · · · · · · · · · · 86
23 Solar · · · · · · · · · · · · · · · · · · · · · · · · · · · · · · · 88
24 Wind · · · · · · · · · · · · · · · · · · · · · · · · · · · · · · · 90
25 Biomass · · · · · · · · · · · · · · · · · · · · · · · · · · · · · 91
26 Renewable Energy Government Incentives · · · · · · · · · 92
27 Conclusion · · · · · · · · · · · · · · · · · · · · · · · · · · · 95
28 Fuel America Now! – Energy Plan · · · · · · · · · · · · · 102
29 President George W. Bush's Energy Plan · · · · · · · · · 113
30 President Barrack Obama's Energy Plan · · · · · · · · · · 116

31  Oil Price and Selected Global Market Events · · · · · · · · · · · · ·118
32  The Challenge · · · · · · · · · · · · · · · · · · · · · · · · · · · · · · 121
33  John F. Kennedy Moon Speech – Rice University · · · · · · · · · · 129
34  Reference · · · · · · · · · · · · · · · · · · · · · · · · · · · · · · · · · 137

# IMPORTANT DEFINITIONS

**Carbon Dioxide, (CO2)** – An important greenhouse gas emitted from Earth into the atmosphere as a result of natural as well as human related events. Human consumption of fossil fuels is a major producer of CO2. The level of atmospheric CO2 appears to directly correlate with the rise and fall of Earth's average temperature.

**Emitter** – Source of atmospheric CO2. Example: Humans exhale CO2.

**Sink** – Captures atmospheric CO2 and sequesters the carbon. Example: Trees inhale CO2, retaining the carbon and releasing the oxygen back into the atmosphere.

**Sequester** – Store or retain carbon and/or CO2 in a permanent or semi-permanent form. Coal is a form of sequestered carbon.

# IMPORTANT NOTE!

In the Reference Section is a list of the graphics appearing in this book including the Internet links for supplementary information. Following these links will provide further insight on the graphics as well as the subject matter being presented. Since the graphics as well as the supporting data and information have been obtained from the U. S. Government's energy and environmental departments, the potential for biased perspectives supporting special agendas should be minimal but not completely absent.

# INTRODUCTION

**Americans are confronted with a conundrum of such magnitude and urgency, the future of mankind, if not already set, will soon be determined by the actions or inactions of America's elected leaders.** Sorry to say, due to misleading information provided by special interest groups and self serving politicians, most Americans cannot grasp the urgency and seriousness of the world's actual energy, economic and environmental circumstances. If middle, working class Americans does not unite and mobilize to create a vibrant, sustainable economy, the future of America, as well as the future mankind, is bleak at best.

> A lifelong heavy smoker experiences significant shortness of breath with minimal exertion. The smoker undergoes a physical which turns up a diagnosis of a lung cancer which is terminal if left untreated. Unfortunately the required treatment is extremely expensive, controversial plus not covered by the smoker's insurance. Without insurance coverage, the doctor believes the smoker cannot afford the treatment. The doctor is confronted with a dilemma: Should the doctor inform the smoker as to the real diagnosis or not? The doctor's professional sources advise of a fantastic new treatment that is just 'over the horizon', which will be affordable and will completely cure the smoker. The doctor, rather than allow the smoker to determine what is in the smoker's best interest; decides to direct the smoker to quit smoking or at a minimum reduce smoking as much as possible. The doctor instructs the smoker that by making this change in life style, the smoker will breathe better and have more energy even though the doctor knows this is not true. The doctor is fully aware the smoker will eventually die without treatment but determines to gamble the smoker's future on the possibility of a new cure that may or may not become available.

(Reference: 2.1)

**The preceding metaphor illustrates how America's leaders are misleading Americans by stating that America must reduce reliance on carbon based fuels to end global warming.** America's leaders must realize the current, historically high level of atmospheric CO2, if left untreated, is far greater than is required to induce a level of climate change, that at best will make Earth extremely inhospitable for human life. Plus, due to the needs of an expanding human population, it is impossible to reduce current and future carbon emissions to a level which will also reduce current atmospheric CO2 levels necessary to reverse global warming.

**Americans must avoid the fantasy of believing world leaders will come together and arrive at a consensus as to the actions required to negate the environmental damage resulting from human activity of the past, present and in the future.** Also, Americans cannot stand by while America's elected leaders, under the pretense of containing global warming, make flawed energy, economic and environmental decisions. **Without the proactive participation by energy focused American voters; the future of America and mankind is bleak at best.**

**No matter what the environmental consequences, make no mistake about it there is no substitute for fossil fuels; not today or in the foreseeable future.** Without the energy and products produced from fossil fuels, life as we know it will cease. **If you think reducing or even eliminating mankind's reliance on fossil fuels will resolve the world's environmental problems, you are wrong. It's just not that simple.**

**Prior to mankind discovering fire, the exchange of carbon between the earth and atmosphere was fundamentally in balance.** When humans discovered fire and over time developed more and more uses for fire, the carbon exchange between the earth and atmosphere was permanently out of balance. Now fast forward to the start of the industrial revolution when carbon emitted into the atmosphere as a consequence of industrial advancements really accelerated. By the time mankind realized the

## INTRODUCTION

environmental impact of ever increasing carbon being dumped into the atmosphere; the carbon in the atmosphere necessary for climate change was in place.

Carbon emitted into the atmosphere takes the form of Carbon Dioxide, ($CO_2$). Since $CO_2$ is such a small component of the atmosphere, (less than .04%), there is considerable controversy as to the actual impact $CO_2$ can have on global temperatures. Notwithstanding the minuscule amount of $CO_2$ in earth's atmosphere, historical atmospheric research and analysis appears to indicate a direct correlation between atmospheric $CO_2$ and the earth's temperature. **Even with a direct cause and effect between $CO_2$ and global temperatures, should Americans panic?** Not according to the Nongovernmental International Panel on Climate Change, (NIPCC).

SECURE OUR SHIP! FUEL AMERICA NOW!

## REPORT OF THE NONGOVERNMENTAL INTERNATIONAL PANEL ON CLIMATE CHANGE

"We donated our time and best efforts to produce this report out of concern that the IPCC, (International Panel on Climate Change) was provoking an irrational fear of anthropogenic global warming based on incomplete and faulty science. **Global warming hype has led to demands for unrealistic efficiency standards for cars, the construction of uneconomic wind and solar energy stations, the establishment of large production facilities for uneconomic biofuels such as ethanol from corn, requirements that electric companies purchase expensive power from so-called 'renewable' energy sources, and plans to sequester, at considerable expense, carbon dioxide emitted from power plants. While there is absolutely nothing wrong with initiatives to increase energy efficiency or diversify energy sources, they cannot be justified as a realistic means to control climate. In addition, policies have been developed that try to hide the huge cost of greenhouse gas controls, such as cap and trade, a Clean Development Mechanism, carbon offsets, and similar scams that enrich a few at the expense of the rest of us.**

Seeing science clearly misused to shape public policies that have the potential to inflict severe economic harm, particularly on low-income groups, we choose to speak up for science at a time when too few people outside the scientific community know what is happening, and too few scientists who know the truth have the will or the platforms to speak out against the IPCC."

Courtesy of and Published by THE HEARTLAND INSTITUTE

(Reference: 2.3)

# INTRODUCTION

**The problem with scientists, environmentalists, industrialists and other specialists is the irrepressible predisposition for tunnel vision!** If there is an 'ominous threat' predicted within their specialty, action must be commenced to resolve the undesirable consequence. Little, if any, consideration is given to the possibility that the 'cure could be worse than the disease'. As American voters, we need to do our best to consider the problem, potential solutions and the probable consequences of those solutions. **Americans must base their political support and vote on logic, not emotions.**

**Rather than get involved in the CO2 cause and effect controversy, examine the potential consequences if mankind makes the wrong choice.** If mankind decides that increased atmospheric CO2 is not the cause of global warming; then does nothing, and is incorrect, the world will likely warm up to the point that much of the earth will no longer support human life. If mankind determines that the level of atmospheric CO2 does control earth's temperature and is incorrect; there will be a significant waste of financial, material and labor resources but human life should continue as nature cycles back to a cooler phase. Logic seems to indicate the second option to be in the best interest of mankind.

**What can Americans do since there is no way world leaders will arrive at a consensus which will resolve the crucial energy and environmental challenge confronting mankind?** The destiny of Americans, as well as mankind, is bleak unless: (1) Americans understand the correlation between energy, the economy and the environment. (2) Develop a plan that can resolve America's energy, economic and environmental dilemma. (3) Vote for leaders that agree to support and implement the energy, economic and environment plan designed to strengthen America to combat global warming. **As Americans, we cannot afford to allow America's future to be determined by special interest groups, self serving politicians and above all, not to leaders of foreign countries.**

**Without the support of other countries, is America starting down the path of isolationism?** No! America must take on the position of world leadership in the battle for the survival of mankind. America will be demonstrating the leadership as well as the determination necessary to overcome the negative impact of world overpopulation. **By reviving America's economy, Americans will be able to fund, develop and implement the technology required to make a better life for all mankind.**

**You may be pro-environment or pro-energy; once you read this book you will realize energy, the economy and environment are much like a 3 leg stool.** The stool relies on all three legs to be functional. America is that stool. Once Americans understand the connection between energy, the economy and environment, a viable energy policy can be developed that will enhance the future of America and the world. Upon completion of this book you will have gained insight into how for decades, America's elected leaders have mismanaged America's energy resources. As a direct result of this abuse of responsibility; many Americans have had to suffer pointless economic hardships and sacrifices.

**On the surface, some of the proposed solutions put forth in this book will appear to be counter-intuitive; however the information and conclusions presented in this book are the result of years of research and reflection.** Before you disregard the proposals put forth in this book, ask yourself if the route America is currently pursuing is going to meet the needs of the average American? Also, how can America's elected leadership risk the future of Americans on energy methods and technology that does not exist and may never exist? Do you think it may well be the time to rethink America's energy, economic and environmental strategy?

**As the reader, you may be a Democrat, Republican, Liberal or Conservative, you will gain insight into the correlation between energy, the economy and the environment; which will alter your stance on what America must do for Americans plus combat global warming.**

# AMERICA, ENERGY, ENVIRONMENT & POLITICS

**Should concern for global warming be the fundamental basis for America's energy, economic and environmental decisions?** Should America ignore its substantial fossil fuel resources as a response to global warming? Must Americans submit to draconian changes in lifestyle to save the environment? How will the government's current and impending energy decisions impact the lives and futures of most Americans? Does anyone have an idea of what will be the energy of the future? These are only a few of the important questions that must be addressed before an energy policy beneficial to most Americans can be developed.

**Unknown by many Americans is the fact America does not have a comprehensive and/or cohesive energy policy.** Due to the current disproportionate and conflicting influence of environmental extremists, major energy company lobbyists and other special interest groups on America's elected leaders; America will not develop a meaningful energy policy. What can American voters do to offset the manipulative influence these groups have on America's elected leaders? First, Americans must become energy literate and know why they believe as they do about America's energy options. Second, Americans must put aside their emotions, politics and personal biases, focusing on America's energy options and consider an energy policy that is in the best interest of most Americans. Next, American voters must provide elected leaders with a clear set of 'sailing orders' for developing a realistic energy policy. Finally, hold individual politicians accountable for their support or lack of support for the energy policy they were elected to enact.

**No doubt about it, energy is the foundation of America's economy.** Abundant, stable, secure, and affordable energy will support an American economy that will provide jobs and opportunities for all Americans. A robust American economy will allow America to lead the fight to control global warming. Without abundant, stable, secure and affordable energy

America's economy will continue to flounder with Americans struggling to support themselves and their families. **Without a strong, stable America, how will mankind have a chance of conquering global warming?**

**If politically moderate Americans do not get actively involved in creating an energy policy, energy costs will continue to fluctuate wildly and increase exponentially.** Increasing energy costs will cause the primal struggle for survival to increasingly become the focus of more and more Americans; resulting in an escalating conflict between less affluent and wealthier Americans. Forget about the Government's price indices and unemployment rates; since these numbers do not accurately reflect the economic issues confronting most Americans. Day to day living expenses are increasing rapidly; plus jobs with a future are becoming more difficult for businesses to create. A trend that will continue until America develops an energy policy that is in the best interest of most Americans.

**What can rational Americans do?** Extremists on both ends of the political spectrum have gained control of America's two major political parties. Regardless of which party gains majority control of Congress and the Presidency, the opposing party will do its best to thwart most, if not all, the legislation and efforts of the politically stronger party. Sorry to say, with extremists controlling each party, this situation is not likely to change. Believe it or not, due to the fact both political parties are controlled by extremists, the current political power struggle may be in the best interest of America.

**How can the current political gridlock be in the best interest of America?** Refer back to when Congress was voting on President Obama's medical care bill? The Speaker of the House instructed members to pass a health care bill "so that you can find out what is in it"! Is this how Americans expect their elected representatives to pass major legislation? It doesn't matter whether the health bill is beneficial for Americans or not.

The important point is that with a single party in control of Congress and the Presidency, legislation was passed with no one having an understanding of the benefits, costs and economic impact of the legislation!

**The real threat for Americans is even more ominous!** America's governing body has deteriorated to the point where America is governed primarily by 3 individuals: The President, the Speaker of the House and the Senate Majority Leader. For example, the Republican controlled House passes a budget plan and the Democrat Leader of the Senate refuses to allow the Senate to consider the bill. Then the Democrat controlled Senate passes an Immigration bill which the Republican Speaker of the House refuses to allow the Republican controlled House consider. Clearly, this situation cannot continue. If our elected representatives cannot stand up for Americans, it is time for Americans to stand up for themselves.

**Americans can regain control of America.** How? Americans need to forget about supporting specific political parties and get involved in developing, supporting and promoting solutions designed for the benefit of most, if not all, Americans. Then hold elected leaders accountable for the success or failure of the proposed solutions.

**When reasonable people understand the problem plus the risks and rewards of potential solutions, a realistic decision can be made.** Regrettably, the people we elect to lead us find it difficult, if not impossible, to represent Americans in a rational manner due to party politics; plus the pressure of well financed special interest groups and lobbyists. Rational Americans must make every effort to offset the inappropriate influence political party leaders and special interest groups have on elected leaders.

**America has many problems that need to be resolved.** Sadly, it is impossible to solve all of America's problems simultaneously. As with the saying: 'A journey of a thousand miles begins with a single step.' Americans need to determine what the first step should be. What 'step' will be the most beneficial to the majority of Americans? The answer should be obvious: The step that creates opportunities for Americans to provide for themselves and their families in a safe and secure environment. In other words, most Americans want a robust economy with a vibrant job market.

**What 'step' will have the greatest impact on employment in America?** The answer is quite simple: Energy! More specifically, abundant and cheap energy! Regrettably, the course of action for meeting America's energy needs is one of, if not the most controversial topics confronting America today. Once Americans understand the political pressure of extremists on both sides of the energy debate; it is easy to understand why America's economy continues to flounder without a meaningful energy policy.

**If America's economy is to flourish, a sensible energy policy, immune to changes in political power, must be developed and enacted.** There will have to be give and take on both sides of the energy and environment struggle. As Americans, we need to accept the fact that unless we make our expectations known to our elected representatives, it is extremely unlikely that America will ever have a meaningful energy policy. As Americans, we also must accept the responsibility to understand America's energy options as well as the problems associated with various energy resources, methods and technology. As Americans, we need to provide our elected representatives with a 'clear set of sailing orders'. In other words, the basics of an energy plan that will create and support an economy which will provide the financial resources required to undo the environmental damage that threatens the very existence of mankind.

**Is it possible that implementing an action in response to a problem could be worse than taking no action at all?** America's leaders are forcing Americans to accept higher cost fossil fuels plus many other sacrifices under the pretension that by reducing America's 'carbon footprint' global warming can be reversed. The fact remains there is already enough $CO_2$ in the atmosphere to make planet earth extremely inhospitable for humans. By misdirecting the public's attention on reducing present and future CO2 emissions, the real problem of excessive CO2 currently in the atmosphere, is ignored. If mankind is to survive, the existing level of atmospheric CO2 must be reduced. This is a fact that must be accepted and with a bit of luck, it is not too late to put into action the measures required to monitor and control atmospheric CO2.

**According to a Wall Street Journal article published October 3, 2013, America has or will shortly become the World's largest producer of energy.** Another article published by the Wall Street Journal on October 5, 2013, describes how States are making energy deals with aluminum plants to influence the aluminum companies to continue employing Americans. Unfortunately, other Americans will be required to pay higher utility bills to underwrite the energy deals required to retain the jobs for workers at the aluminum plants. Is this the way America should be sustaining jobs? Under current political and energy conditions, the answer is YES. But, there is a better way for America to create and sustain jobs which will be clearly illustrated shortly.

A follow up article in the Wall Street Journal published October 18, 2013, titled 'Aluminum Glut Claims Major Smelter in Ohio' states: "Power typically accounts for between a quarter and a third of the smelter's operating costs. With aluminum prices slipping to under $1,800 a ton from over $2,600 two years ago, aluminum production has migrated to low cost energy areas like the Middle East and Iceland,". The company previously employed nearly 1,200 Americans. Can Americans continue to ignore America's abundant energy resources?

**Providing the insight required to develop a 'clear set of sailing orders' is the focus of this book.** To develop a 'clear set of sailing orders', Americans must have a fundamental understanding of the energy options, including the benefits and problems of each energy alternative. As rational

Americans, we cannot afford to remain silent. We need to make our wishes and expectations known to our elected leaders. **America will never have the stable economy and security expected by all Americans without a realistic energy policy.**

# WHY IS ENERGY SO IMPORTANT?

World population milestones. **Source:** United Nations Secretariat, Department of Economic and Social Affairs, *The World At Six Billion* (1999), p. 8.

| World population reached: | Year | Time to add 1 billion |
|---|---|---|
| 1 billion | 1804 | |
| 2 billion | 1927 | 123 years |
| 3 billion | 1960 | 33 years |
| 4 billion | 1974 | 14 years |
| 5 billion | 1987 | 13 years |
| 6 billion | 1999 | 12 years |

(Reference: 4.1)

Look close at the table. **In 1804, it is estimated world population reached 1 billion people.** Due to the Industrial Revolution along with major advancements in medicine and improved agricultural productivity, it only took 123 years for the world's population to double. **By 2012, the world's population was estimated at more than 7 billion.** If it has not already been attained, at what point will the human population exceed Earth's capacity to sustain human life?

**What about population growth in America?** In 1790, the United States conducted its first census. There were 13 states with a total population of less than 4 million people. This amounted to approximately 4.5 people per square mile. Also, the Industrial Revolution was beginning in America. By 1810 America had added 4 states and the population had almost doubled. The population per square mile actually decreased to 4.3 people per square mile. A hundred years later, according to the 1910 census, America now had 46 states with America's population increasing to more than 90 million people. This amounted to approximately 26 people per square mile. The most recent census in 2010 puts America's population at slightly less than 310 million people. This breaks down to more than 87 people per square mile.

In a study titled *Food, Land, Population and the U.S. Economy*, it was estimated the maximum U.S. population for a sustained economy and avert disaster at 200 million. If this study is correct, America should reduce its population by more than a third with the world population reduced by at least two thirds! Obviously, such a reduction in population will not occur without some sort of tragedy.

**The real problem confronting America today is adapting to a world that is increasingly over populated.** Other issues such as global warming attributed to increased atmospheric $CO_2$ are really symptoms of over population. Fortunately, if the 'experts' are correct, the world population growth rate is decreasing. Many of the most affluent countries of the world, including America, have population growth below the 2.1 births per woman, (bpw), required to sustain a population. As stated, America's rate of population growth is less than the required 2.1 bpw but due to current immigration laws, America's population will continue to grow.

**Unfortunately, many of the less affluent countries have growth rates significantly greater than the 2.1 bpw rate required to maintain a consistent population level.** The imbalance in growth rates between the affluent and less affluent countries is creating an increasing population of under nourished people. At the same time as some countries become more affluent the demand on Earth's limited resources, especially energy, increases exponentially.

**According to the U.S Energy Information Agency, (EIA):** "The *International Energy Outlook 2013, (IEO2013)*, projects world energy consumption will grow by 56 percent between 2010 and 2040." Additionally the EIA states: "Fossil fuels continue to supply almost 80 percent of world energy use through 2040." Interestingly, the EIA states: "Coal use grows faster than petroleum and other liquid fuel use until after 2030, mostly because of increases in China's consumption of coal".

**What does the world's population mean to America?** Since energy costs impact virtually every product required to sustain the human population, America must make a crucial choice: (1) America continues on the current course requiring most Americans to accept a deteriorating life style as a result of increasing energy costs, dwindling energy supplies and unreliable availability. (2) America takes the steps required to utilize America's abundant and affordable energy resources to maintain or even improve the life style of most Americans.

**If America continues to ignore its energy resources, the life style of Americans will continue to worsen while the cost of living rapidly escalates.** America's military strength will weaken significantly, placing the security of Americans in jeopardy. Global warming will continue unchecked and at some point nature will prevail in making the changes necessary to bring the environment back in balance.

**If America develops its energy resources, America could:** (1) Develop a strong economy that will provide the jobs and opportunities Americans deserve and expect. (2) Maintain a strong military that will insure the security of Americans. (3) Provide the rest of the world with the products and services required to sustain and improve life. (4) Totally reverse America's balance in trade by eliminating oil purchases and increasing products sold to other countries. (5) Research, develop and implement the technology necessary to monitor and control the CO2 in the earth's atmosphere, (eliminate the global warming threat).

No matter what America does, the undeniable fact is; if humans do not take steps to control world population, the world population will continue to grow until nature decides enough is enough. Pending nature's defensive action, the world is going to need more and more energy to sustain the increasing human population. Fossil fuels will continue to be consumed to support humanity and without a method to control atmospheric CO2; simultaneously result in the end of civilization as we know it. **That's the conundrum confronting America today: How to meet the needs of Americans without bringing about the ultimate destruction of mankind.**

# CARBON BASED LIFE AND CO2

Life on earth is referred to as 'carbon based' due to the fact that carbon is the key element in every life form on earth. The total amount of carbon on earth and in the atmosphere is fixed. Carbon bonds readily with other elements moving dynamically and freely between living organisms and a variety of inorganic compounds. CO2 enters the atmosphere through emitters and returns to the earth via CO2 sinks. If CO2 is moving from the earth, into the atmosphere and returned to earth in balance or equal amounts, there are no problems. Troubles begin when the flow of CO2 into the atmosphere gets out of balance with CO2 returned to earth.

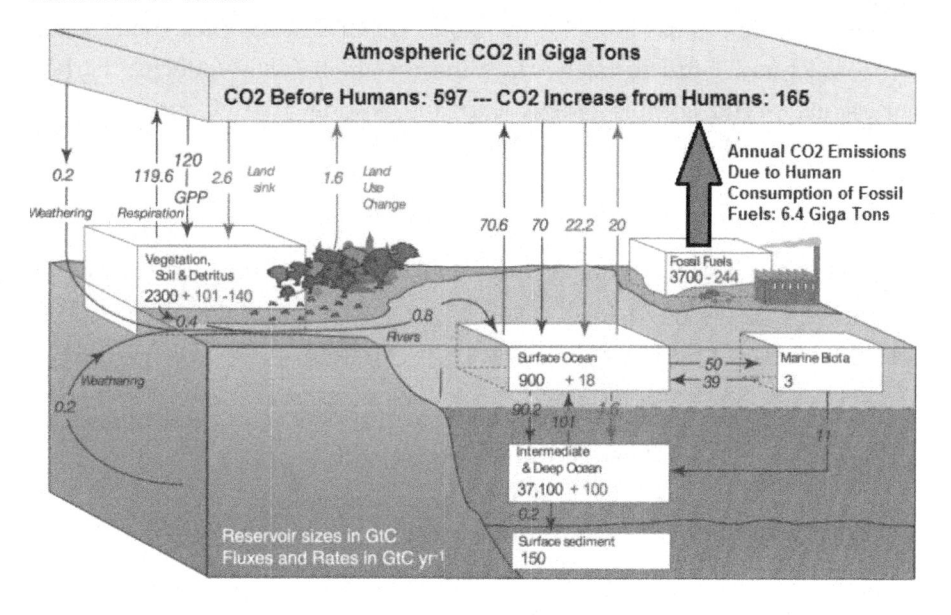

(Reference: 5.1)

The preceding image, (Reference 5.1), illustrates the flow of CO2 between the atmosphere and earth. The arrows pointing up represent CO2 emitted into the atmosphere, (emitters). The arrows pointing down denote CO2 being absorbed by the earth, (sinks or receptors). Note the flow of fossil fuels accountable to humans for transportation and industry. Only a fraction of the CO2 emissions attributable to human consumption can be attributed to America. As other nations, such as China and India, strive to modernize their way of living, the CO2 emissions will continue to increase with the overall percentage attributable to America decreasing. If global warming is to be reversed, America must rethink its energy and environmental policies.

Fossil fuels contain carbon that has been sequestered for millions of years. The burning of fossil fuels releases the previously sequestered carbon into the atmosphere in the form of CO2. Environmentalists want to decrease or even eliminate the use of fossil fuels due to the CO2 emissions. Environmentalists use global warming as the justification for their assault on fossil fuels. Unfortunately, the time in which solely reducing carbon emissions would combat global warming is long gone. Containing and reversing global warming will be considerably more difficult than just reducing current and future carbon emissions.

As you can see from the table below, different fossil fuels emit different amounts of CO2 based on the energy produced. The table indicates the <u>pounds</u> of CO2 emitted per <u>million</u> BTU of energy produced.

| | |
|---|---|
| Coal (anthracite) | 228.6 |
| Coal (bituminous) | 205.7 |
| Coal (lignite) | 215.4 |
| Coal (sub-bituminous) | 214.3 |
| Diesel fuel & heating oil | 161.3 |
| Gasoline | 157.2 |
| Propane | 139.0 |
| Natural gas | 117.0 |

(Reference: 5.2)

The amount of CO2 produced is directly related to the carbon content of the fossil fuel. The energy produced is primarily a function of the Carbon, (C), and/or Hydrogen, (H), combining with Oxygen, (O), during combustion. The amount of energy produced by fossil fuels can be reduced by water content plus other elements such as Sulfur.

As the table shows, anthracite coal produces the most CO2 due to the fact that it consists of as much as 98 percent carbon. Anthracite coal accounts for about 1 percent of the earth's coal reserves. The bituminous, lignite and sub-bituminous contain less carbon than anthracite and produce less energy per unit consumed.

The fossil fuel producing the least CO2 is natural gas. Natural gas primarily consists of Methane, ($CH_4$), which has a high amount of hydrogen content, allowing natural gas to produce the least amount of CO2 per unit of energy of all the fossil fuels. If the energy decision is based solely on CO2 emissions, Natural gas is the obvious choice. But if natural gas is exported and/or used exclusively as an energy source, America's natural gas reserves will be rapidly depleted. Americans must make sure America's vast energy resources are used in the most efficient manner possible.

**According to the U. S. Energy Information Agency, (EIA):** Fossil fuels are generally combusted for the purpose of producing energy useful for heat and work. During the combustion process, the C stored in the fuels is oxidized and emitted as CO2 and smaller amounts of other gases, including methane, (CH4), carbon dioxide, (CO), and non-methane volatile organic compounds, (NMVOCs). These non-CO2 gases are emitted as a byproduct of incomplete fuel combustion, but are, for the most part, eventually oxidized to CO2 in the atmosphere. Therefore, it is taken for granted that all of the carbon in fossil fuels used to produce energy is eventually converted to atmospheric CO2.

# GLOBAL WARMING DATA, STATISTICS & RESEARCH

In the United States, most information on global warming will be supplied by government agencies or government funded research. A major supplier of global warming data and statistics is the National Oceanic and Atmospheric Administration, (NOAA). NOAA operates more than 8,000 weather stations. NOAA also operates 1221 stations in the United States' Historical Climatology Network (USHCN).

Is there evidence that the earth is warming, other than temperature data and statistics? Yes. According to NOAA lakes and river ice is melting earlier and forming later in the year. Plants are blooming earlier. A variety of birds, fish, mammals and plants are expanding their range northward and higher in the mountains. Based on information provided by NOAA, global warming or climate change is occurring; it's the cause of climate change that may be debatable.

According to Fox News, between 2011 and 2013, NOAA closed approximately 600 weather stations that were problematic or unnecessary. This was done after a long campaign by an outspoken critic condemning NOAA for possibly using unreliable data. Evidently, NOAA agrees since it states the closing of the stations will improve the gathering of weather data.

If the weather data collected from the sites closed by NOAA had been reporting data that did not support the global warming theory, would NOAA need a critic to prompt the closing of the weather stations? Hopefully not but this also leads to another question. Since substantial global warming research is funded by the government, what would happen to researchers creating global warming reports that do not support the government's position? Again, hopefully nothing but there is potential for bias due to perceived or actual pressure to support the government's stance on global warming.

The locations of NOAA's weather stations are important. If a weather station has been reporting for years and then a significant construction project or other significant change occurs in close proximity, the weather station's future data reporting could be meaningfully distorted. Even though NOAA states that it has statistical methods to adjust the data, can the data be adjusted accurately enough to not distort the overall historical reporting? Since mathematicians assert that equations can be written for anything; the continuity might be sustainable but the doubt and debate will continue to linger.

According to the NOAA critic credited for being the catalyst for the closing of the 600 weather stations; if only the weather data obtained at 'pristine' sites is analyzed the temperature increase between 1979 and 2008 was 1.1 degrees Fahrenheit. If the data for all the weather stations is included in analysis the temperature increase was 1.7 degrees Fahrenheit. The difference between the two analyses using the complete set of weather data results in almost 155% temperature increase over an analysis including only the 'pristine' sites. Is it possible that the weather data cannot be corrected for distortion? If the comparison is correct, it appears that the statistical adjustments are not working.

NOAA should have nothing to gain by intentionally distorting the weather data it collects. It's important for NOAA to provide government officials and concerned Americans with as accurate weather information as is possible. It is the responsibility of elected government officials to take the appropriate action based on the weather data NOAA provides. The 'appropriate action' is the crux of the global warming debate.

Anyone that has lived for an extended period near the coast, around the mountains and in many other locations will likely acknowledge there are some significant weather changes occurring. The question becomes is the change a normal weather cycle or a result of human activity? The obvious position of the government and environmentalists is the change is caused by human consumption of fossil fuels. Whether the government and environmentalists are correct is the subject of debate.

Americans need to get involved in the global warming controversy. Americans cannot rely solely on climate change information provided by any single source. The idea that the only solution to global warming is to reduce America's reliance on fossil fuels to decrease CO2 emissions is at a minimum questionable. At worse, reducing America's reliance on fossil fuels could end America's way of life and do nothing to end global warming.

Americans need to question the information supplied by and supporting the position of environmentalists, oil companies, special interest groups and governmental organizations. With the advent of the Internet, virtually everyone can verify information on practically any subject including global warming. The information included and conclusions presented in this book are no exception.

# IS THERE A CO2 AND GLOBAL WARMING CAUSE AND EFFECT RELATIONSHIP?

**Carbon Dioxide Concentration and Temperature Anomaly**

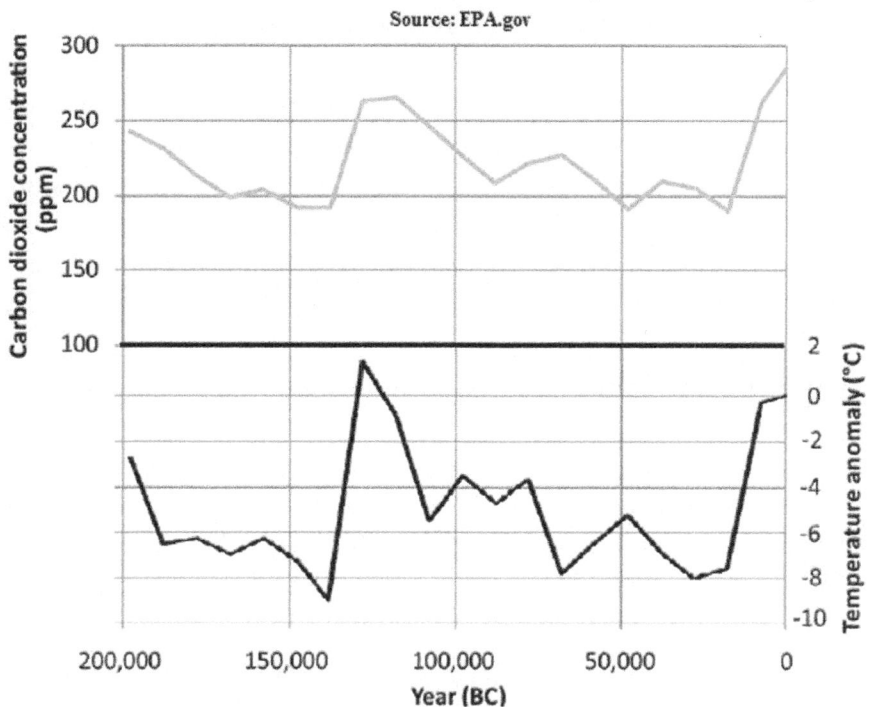

Source: EPA.gov

(Reference: 7.1)

The Carbon Dioxide Concentration and Temperature Anomaly chart above was created from data gathered from drilling into ice formations that have existed for thousands of years. Air samples locked into the ice were analyzed for chemical content. The top graph indicates changes in CO2 in earth's atmosphere over the last 200,000 years. (The complete chart includes the last 800,000 years.) The bottom graph represents the temperature change as the CO2 content of the atmosphere changed. If the inferred temperature analysis is correct there is a correlation between the level of CO2 in the atmosphere and the earth's temperature.

**Look closer, there is more to gain from the chart.** Note that approximately 120,000 to 140,000 years ago there was a CO2 situation analogous to what the earth is currently experiencing. But just as importantly note the fact that the earth's atmosphere has been increasing in CO2 for the past 20,000 years as has the earth's average temperature. In other words global warming has been underway for much longer than the 150 years since the start of the Industrial Revolution. (The Industrial Revolution appears to have significantly accelerated increase in atmospheric CO2 but, fortunately for mankind, earth's average temperature is increasing at a much slower rate.)

The most important question which must be answered: Is the temperature increase a result of the increase in CO2 in the atmosphere or is the increase in atmospheric CO2 a result of the increase in temperature? The answer to this question may be debatable but there is one indisputable fact that makes a strong argument for CO2 being the cause of earth's temperature changes. That is the fact that CO2 does absorb the sun's infrared radiation, (IR), and later release the IR in the form thermal energy, qualifying CO2 as a greenhouse gas. Without atmospheric CO2 the earth would be a giant ball of ice. Based on the 'Carbon Dioxide Concentration and Temperature Anomaly' chart, it appears humans thrive when the atmospheric CO2 level is in the 250 to 280 ppm, (parts per million).

What is interesting is how little of the atmosphere consists of CO2. The primary component of air is Nitrogen at approximately 78 percent followed by Oxygen at nearly 21 percent. These two elements account for more than 99 percent of earth's atmosphere! CO2 accounts for less than .04 percent of earth's atmosphere! It's amazing that such a small component of air can have such a significant impact on earth's climate.

## IS THERE A CO2 AND GLOBAL WARMING CAUSE AND EFFECT RELATIONSHIP?

**What if all the nations of the world abandoned fossil fuels?** Ignore the economic and social issues and focus only on global warming. Would global warming be eliminated? According to most global warming information provided to the public, the 'politically correct' answer is yes. But is yes the correct answer?

At the start of the Industrial Revolution the atmospheric $CO_2$ content is estimated at approximately 280 ppm, (parts per million air particles). As of June, 2013, according to NOAA, (National Oceanic and Atmospheric Administration), the atmospheric $CO_2$ content was 398.58 ppm.

Looking back at the period between 120,000 and 140,000 years ago, there was an increase in $CO_2$ of approximately 60 to 70 ppm. During the same period, the average temperature appears to have increased by 9 to 10 degrees Centigrade, (16.2 to 18 degrees Fahrenheit). Since the beginning of the Industrial Revolution the atmospheric $CO_2$ has increased by more than 118 ppm. The temperature change is nowhere close to what occurred 120,000 to 140,000 years ago with only a 60 to 70 ppm increase in $CO_2$. Is there really a correlation between atmospheric $CO_2$ and the earth's temperature?

Historically, the increase in atmospheric $CO_2$ has occurred over thousands of years. Is it possible that an increase in the earth's average temperature has not been able to keep up with the rapid increase in atmospheric $CO_2$? NOAA uses the electric blanket analogy: Turn up the temperature control and the blanket's temperature does not increase immediately, it takes some time. Maybe the atmospheric $CO_2$ works the same way. Or are the skeptics correct in their belief that there is no correlation between atmospheric $CO_2$ and the earth's average temperature? Since no one seems able to provide an indisputable answer, what action, if any, should the world take in response to possible global warming?

If global warming is occurring and no action is taken, the future of the human race is bleak at best and non-existent at worse. If global warming is not occurring and efforts to reduce atmospheric CO2 are implemented, a significant investment of money, material and time has been wasted but the human race continues. Logic seems to indicate that the second choice is best choice.

Returning to the question: What if all the nations of the world abandoned fossil fuels? Would global warming be eliminated? As previously stated, the consensus between environmentalists and politicians is that atmospheric CO2 has increased significantly since the start of the Industrial Revolution. The implication is that this increase in CO2 is entirely due to mankind's increasing use of fossil fuels. There is no doubt that consuming fossil fuels increase atmospheric CO2 but little has been said about the exploding human population that has occurred over the same time period.

As stated in the previous section, in 1750, the start of the Industrial Revolution, the world's population was less than 800 million people. At the start of 2013, the total world's population is estimated at more than 7 billion people. Now consider every person emits 1,000 pounds of CO2 into the atmosphere just by breathing. Add to this the land that must be cleared of trees and other vegetation, which had absorbed CO2 from the atmosphere and released oxygen, but had to be cleared to house and feed the increased population. The imbalance between carbon emitters and sinks grows wider. Now add the tilling, planting and processing of grains, vegetables and fruits that must be produced to feed the growing human population. On top of this add in the animals that have to be fed and processed as food. Clearly, the imbalance between carbon emitters and sinks would exist with or without fossil fuels.

Look closely at the *'Carbon Dioxide Concentration and Temperature Anomaly'* chart and note that at no point in the last 200,000 years has the atmospheric CO2 approached its 2013 level of 398.58 ppm. Think about it: At no point in the last 200,000 years has the atmospheric CO2 approached the 2013 level of 398.58 ppm! (Important: On May 9, 2013 NOAA, atop the Mauna Loa Observatory on the Big Island of Hawaii, the atmospheric CO2 measurements did exceed 400 ppm!) If CO2 is responsible for past temperature changes, the damage has been done. According to what the *'Carbon Dioxide Concentration and Temperature Anomaly"* chart shows for the period between 120,000 and 140,000 years in the past, if action is not taken to reduce the current level of CO2, the world can expect average temperatures to increase by as much as 20 degrees Centigrade, (36 degrees Fahrenheit).

**An important point that must be stated:** There is high probability that as atmospheric CO2 increases Earth's average temperatures <u>do not</u> increase proportionally. The statistical evidence indicates that at some point, Earth's average temperature rate of increase slows as atmospheric CO2 levels increase. Eventually, little or no temperature change will be the direct result of increased atmospheric CO2.

Over time, how bad could global warming get? In 2013 temperatures in the Southwest U.S. exceeded 115 degrees Fahrenheit. Now add 36 degrees Fahrenheit and the temperatures could exceed 151 degrees Fahrenheit! (The 36 degrees Fahrenheit is the maximum projected temperature increase due to <u>current</u> atmospheric CO2 levels.) In a significant portion of the U.S., temperatures in excess of 100 degrees in the summer are not unusual. Again add 36 degrees and the situation becomes catastrophic. Literally, a large portion of the U.S. and the world will become inhabitable if temperatures increase proportionate to the increase in atmospheric CO2.

> **Richard Norris, Professor of Paleobiology and Curator, SIO Geological Collections, Scripps Institution of Oceanography states:** "The last time Earth saw 400 ppm CO2 in the atmosphere about 3-4 million years back, there were camels and forests in the Arctic, the tropics were locked in a near constant el Nino -- the kind that typically floods the western U.S. -- and large expanses of the U.S. East Coast, Florida and the Gulf States were underwater. Still, we are not going to 'go back to the future' overnight since it takes millennia to melt the ice that would raise global sea levels, but 400 ppm is milestone on the road to a constantly changing world for the foreseeable future... The worst of it is that we are already committed to several thousand years of unsettled climate thanks to our approximately about 150 years of carbon pollution."

(Reference: 7.2)

According to Mr. Norris' statement, the climate change situation appears hopeless but it is not. Devastatingly high temperatures will not occur overnight but there will be significant changes in weather patterns that could result in major adjustments in mankind's way of life. Believe it or not there could be a constructive aspect for the level of atmospheric CO2 being the primary basis for changes in global temperatures. Atmospheric CO2 can be captured and converted into products and elements valuable to humans. Additionally, excess atmospheric CO2 can be sequestered, (buried deep into the earth), if necessary.

The development of the technology required to control atmospheric CO2 is going to require a substantial investment of financial resources, material and time. Luckily, it appears that Nature is allowing mankind time to take corrective action. Nature could allow humans hundreds of years to develop and implement the technology required to correct atmospheric CO2 level. It's up to Americans to commit the required financial resources, materials and labor to control atmospheric CO2. It is highly unlikely any other country will or can make the commitment required to prevent an ecological disaster that could eliminate the human race.

Courtesy of NOAA.

Climate change is expressed in many ways – e.g., drought, increased temperatures, altered storm patterns and precipitation rates, increased glacier melting, etc.

(Reference: 7.3)

Significant time will be required to overcome the climate change occurring due to the current high levels of atmospheric CO2. During this period of time, Americans will need to adjust to the changing climate. Guess What? It's going to take money, lots of money, to minimize the negative impact of climate change. There will be droughts, storms, heat and other events that do not normally occur in different areas of the world. Adjustments will have to be made in the ways Americans live. Farming will require major changes. All of which will require financial resources which will only be available with a strong economy.

As previously stated, America must lead the effort to reduce the current level of atmospheric CO2. There is no other country that can assume the leadership role. America has the required natural resources plus the research, business and social structure necessary for the innovations necessary to monitor and control atmospheric CO2. It's up to politically moderate Americans to make sure America's political leaders provide the required support and regulations. The politically extreme Americans, both left and right wing, will do everything possible to promote their agendas which could prevent real action to monitor and control atmospheric CO2 from being implemented.

Mankind must develop the technology that will allow the atmosphere to maintain the appropriate CO2 levels that will create the temperatures most advantageous for human life. Imagine what a major volcanic eruption could do to current atmospheric CO2 levels! Controlling CO2 or other elements in the atmosphere may seem unattainable but controlling green house gas content may appear more realistic when you consider all the technological advances that have occurred in the last 50 to 100 years.

The real environmental issue is that there is a narrow range of atmospheric CO2 which humans thrive. As previously stated and illustrated in the *'Carbon Dioxide Concentration and Temperature Anomaly'* chart, note that humans appear to have prospered when the atmospheric CO2 content is between 250 to 280 ppm. This is the apparent range of CO2 levels for the last 10,000 years until the Industrial Revolution.

Year to year there will be periods of time that global warming will appear to be over or just a hoax. Climate change will not occur in a steady trend. There will be years in which winter may be colder than normal. There will be summers that are cooler than normal. Climate change must be monitored over decades where these temperature swings will begin to develop a trend.

As previously stated, if climate change is not occurring due to increased atmospheric CO2, mankind must error on the safe side. The other side of

## IS THERE A CO2 AND GLOBAL WARMING CAUSE AND EFFECT RELATIONSHIP?

the coin is that climate change is the result of increased atmospheric CO2 and mankind does nothing. The result of inaction could be disastrous for human life.

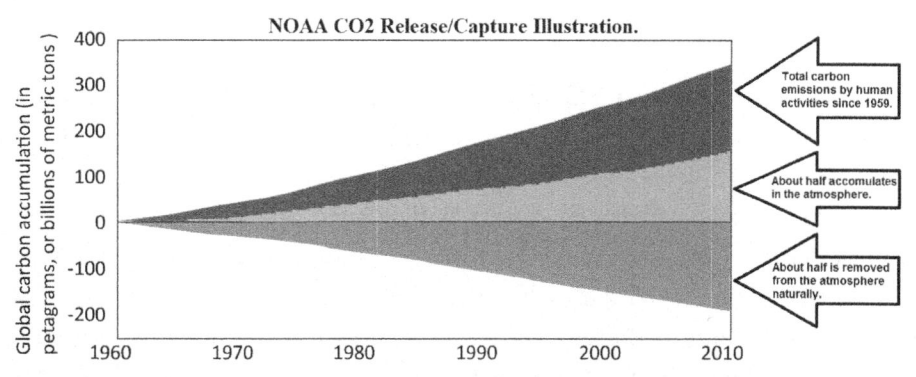

**NOAA CO2 Release/Capture Illustration.**

- Total carbon emissions by human activities since 1959.
- About half accumulates in the atmosphere.
- About half is removed from the atmosphere naturally.

As carbon emissions by human activities have increased, some carbon has stayed in the atmosphere and some has been absorbed by natural "sinks" on land and in the oceans. Natural sinks, including land ecosystems and the oceans, remove about half of the carbon emitted by human activities back out of the atmosphere. Note: The graph depicts carbon accumulation, which is proportional to carbon dioxide accumulation.

(Reference: 7.4)

As the preceding chart from NOAA, (National Oceanic and Atmospheric Administration), points out, regardless of the amount of carbon released into the atmosphere by human activity, half the carbon will be returned to earth! What does this mean? Maybe nature is adapting to the effects resulting from mankind's overpopulation. Can nature continue to absorb half of mankind's CO2 emissions? If so, will there be additional environmental problems which must be corrected?

Some final questions: **Is there a point at which earth's atmosphere will become CO2 saturated?** There could be an atmospheric CO2 saturation level but it is likely far beyond the current levels of CO2 in the atmosphere. **How long does CO2 emissions remain in the atmosphere?** According to Mr. Norris, (as quoted in this section), the CO2 could remain in the atmosphere for thousands of years. According to NOAA the CO2 in the atmosphere will remain approximately 100 years. Obviously, no one knows the answer to this question.

**As the atmospheric CO2 level increases does global warming increase proportionally?** Due to the delay between the increase in atmospheric CO2 levels and Earth's average temperature change, this is a difficult question to answer. Additionally, there appears to be an increase in the temperature in deeper ocean waters as atmospheric CO2 increases. Without a doubt, Earth's environment is complex and even environmental scientists will admit there is still much to learn. The important issue remains that due to human activity, the amount of carbon emitted into the atmosphere will continue to exceed the carbon returned to Earth plus the current level of atmospheric CO2 is more than enough to modify Earth's climate to the point Earth will no longer be hospitable for human life.

# WHAT CAN AMERICA DO ABOUT GLOBAL WARMING?

## U.S. CARBON DIOXIDE EMISSIONS, BY SOURCE

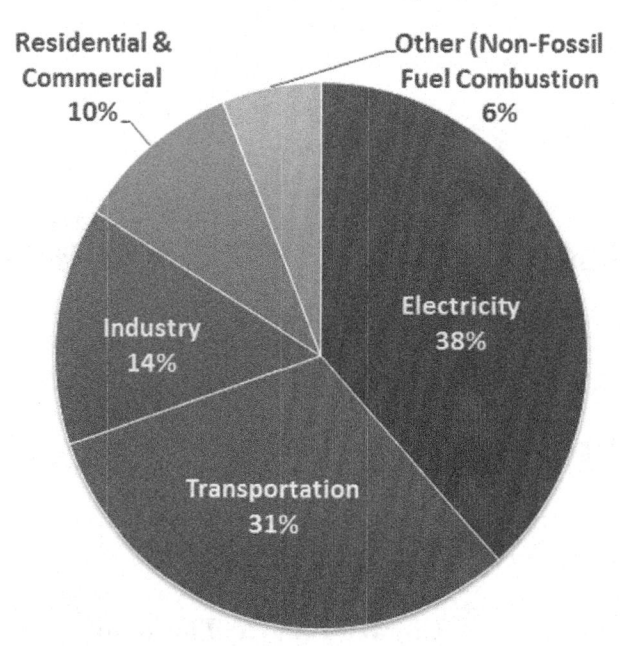

- Residential & Commercial 10%
- Other (Non-Fossil Fuel Combustion) 6%
- Electricity 38%
- Industry 14%
- Transportation 31%

In the United States, since 1990, the management of forests and non-agricultural land has acted as a net sink of $CO_2$, which means that more $CO_2$ is removed from the atmosphere, and stored in plants and trees, than is emitted. This sink offset about 14% of total emissions in 2011.

*According to EPA, (U. S. Environmental Protection Agency), Climate Change Information Site*

(Reference: 8.1)

The EPA chart provides a breakdown of CO2 emissions from human activity in the United States. Note the statement at the bottom of the chart. According to the EPA, America's use of its land captures more CO2 than is emitted. How much more? Approximately 14% of the CO2 emissions from America's human activity are also absorbed by America's forests and other non-agricultural land. Additionally, the EPA estimates America's CO2 emissions should increase by 1.5% between 2005 and 2020. This projection represents a significant reduction in the rate of increase for CO2 emissions in past years.

**Now, take a close look at the following.**

## THE NATIONAL OCEANIC AND ATMOSPHERIC ADMINISTRATION, (NOAA), PUBLISHED AN ARTICLE TITLED:

### GREENHOUSE GASES CONTINUE CLIMBING: 2012 A RECORD YEAR!

Within the article **NOAA** stated: *"Last year, $CO_2$ at the peak of its cycle reached 400 ppm for one month at all eight Arctic sites for the first time."* Plus: *"At this rate of emissions, the global average of $CO_2$ will shortly reach 400 ppm and, within 4 to 5 years"*. **Compare this to The White House's statement:** *"In 2012, U.S. carbon emissions fell to the lowest level in two decades even as the economy continued to grow."* **This is the issue: America can continue to reduce its CO2 emissions but the atmospheric CO2 will continue to grow at nearly 1.5% per year. America must develop the technology to monitor and control atmospheric CO2. There is no way atmospheric CO2 emissions will ever be less than the atmospheric CO2 returned to earth, (CO2 sinks). Unless humans create the technology required to balance CO2 emissions with CO2 sinks, the future of mankind is bleak.**

(Reference: 8.2)

**Recall the prayer: "God, grant me the serenity to accept the things I cannot change, the courage to change the things I can, and the wisdom to know the difference."** Over the last few years, America's $CO_2$ emissions have remained relatively constant while other countries such as China and India have seen significant increases. Evidently, other countries <u>are not</u> following America's lead in limiting $CO_2$ emissions which should result in Americans asking: If other countries continue to consume fossil fuels without concern for the environment, how can America fight global warming single handily?

**Think about it: Earth is the spaceship all mankind relies on for their existence.** Based on America's position of leadership among the countries of the world, America must be viewed as the "bridge or control center of the spaceship earth". Quite simply, the President of the United States is the 'captain of Spaceship Earth' by default. (What other world leader demands the respect comparable to the President of the United States?) **America's President must be above politics and special interest groups.** America's President needs to base decisions on facts, not emotions or predetermined agendas. **Above all, America's President must be a proven leader.**

**America's President is in office to serve Americans and must make energy, economic and security decisions which are in the best interest of most Americans.** America's President must recognize the fact that at the current world population level, more $CO_2$ will continue to be emitted into the atmosphere than can be returned to earth without new technology to monitor and control atmospheric $CO_2$. This fact will not change regardless of any reductions America may make in its $CO_2$ emissions. Furthermore, America's President must accept the fact that without America maintaining a strong, expanding economy, climate change will continue, eventually making spaceship Earth uninhabitable for humans.

**Finally, America's President must accept the fact the future of the world will be determined by what America does or does not do with its vast fossil fuel resources.** Is this belief American arrogance or truth? Consider the facts: No other country has the natural resources plus an economic system designed to encourage individual success. Most Americans realize that problems create opportunities. Opportunities create wealth. The dream of wealth is the driving force for America's economic system. America does control the future of the world!

**Unfortunately, today's America is not the same America that has led the world in the past.** America's Democrat and Republican parties are controlled by extremists and special interest groups. Washington is virtually gridlocked when one party does not control the House of Representatives, Senate and Presidency. As previously stated Congressional gridlock is bad but maybe not as bad as the situation would be with one party controlling Congress and the Presidency.

**American leadership founded on the premise that if America reduces its atmospheric $CO_2$ emissions other countries will follow America's lead is pure fantasy, misleading lies or pure foolhardiness.** Remember: According to the White House, America decreased its atmospheric $CO_2$ emissions in 2012 to the lowest level in 20 years. According to NOAA, (National Oceanic and Atmospheric Administration), the world's atmospheric $CO_2$ level increased at a near record rate in 2012 exceeding 400ppm, (parts per million), for the first time in history. Was the White House statement intentionally misleading?

**The White House's claim of reduced $CO_2$ emissions in 2012 needs to be examined a little closer.** First, any economic growth in 2012 was minimal at best but did America really decrease overall $CO_2$ emissions? The claimed reduction in carbon emissions for 2012 must be challenged. Due to the International agreement not to account for $CO_2$ emissions emitted by renewable fuels, such as ethanol added to gasoline and bio-diesel blended with petroleum diesel, is it possible CO2 emissions in the U. S. did not decrease as publicly announced? Could the reduction in computed CO2 emissions be the result of increased use of bio fuels and not actually a reduction in CO2 emissions? **The White House pronouncement that CO2 emissions decreased in 2012 could be misleading Americans but the global increase in atmospheric CO2 levels in 2012 cannot be disputed.**

**The future of America is up to moderate Americans willing to put aside political alliances plus preconceived energy and environmental opinions and focus on what is in the best interest of most Americans.** There are many important issues confronting America today but none are more important than energy, the economy and the environment. It is challenging to obtain information on global warming and fossil fuels that is not provided by individuals or organizations with a special agenda. It is time to review America's energy options as they impact the lives of most Americans rather than emphasize global warming according to environmentalists or the merits of fossil fuels as presented by the fossil fuel industries.

**Make no mistake OIL is America's primary energy source and the cornerstone of America's economy as well as a significant source for atmospheric CO2.** No other product has a greater impact on the lives of Americans. As oil prices continue to increase, the lives of working Americans become more and more difficult. Unfortunately, most oil price increases have little if anything to do with oil supply and demand. Speculative energy price manipulation must be eliminated as quickly as possible.

**If global warming is to be eliminated, America will have to commence an effort greater than the Manhattan Project during World War 2 and NASA, (National Aeronautics and Space Administration), during the space race.** The future of the human race will be determined by what America does or doesn't do. If global warming is to be eliminated, it is going to require financial resources which will only be available if America creates a solid, rapidly expanding economy. A strong American economy requires immense amounts of affordable and reliable energy. Today, the only proven energy source that can feed the economy required to combat global warming is fossil fuels.

**Increased use of fossil fuels will increase CO2 emissions.** An unfortunate fact but America cannot delay developing the economy required to finance the research, development and implementation of the technology required to eliminate global warming. **Americans cannot continue to hope, wish and fantasize about an energy alternative to fossil fuels.** There is no fossil fuel substitute today and there is no substitute for fossil fuels in the foreseeable future. Furthermore, the CO2 currently in the atmosphere is more than enough to make spaceship Earth extremely uncomfortable for humans. Relying on efforts to reduce additional CO2 emissions to combat global warming, is equivalent to closing the corral gate once the horses are out.

**The first step in the battle against global warming will be to reduce additional atmospheric CO2 emissions from the increased consumption of fossil fuels.** Stationary facilities such as power plants account for a significant amount of CO2 emissions and should be the simplest to modify. Atmospheric CO2 emissions due to transportation will likely be more difficult to control but in no way, impossible to reduce.

**Time is not on the side of mankind.** At some point it will be too late. Americans must concede that atmospheric CO2 is the cause of global warming. Also, Americans must acknowledge the fact the atmosphere as it is today contains more than enough CO2 to create an environment that would be extremely difficult, if not impossible for human life to continue.

**Americans need to prepare for climate change due to current atmospheric CO2 levels.** Until atmospheric CO2 levels can be reduced, there is going to be changes in climate. America will require a strong economy to make the adjustments necessary for the climate change that is now occurring and that will likely accelerate as atmospheric CO2 increases. **America must focus on correcting the damage that has been done to the atmosphere by developing the technology required to monitor and control atmospheric CO2 levels.**

# AMERICA'S ENERGY OPTIONS

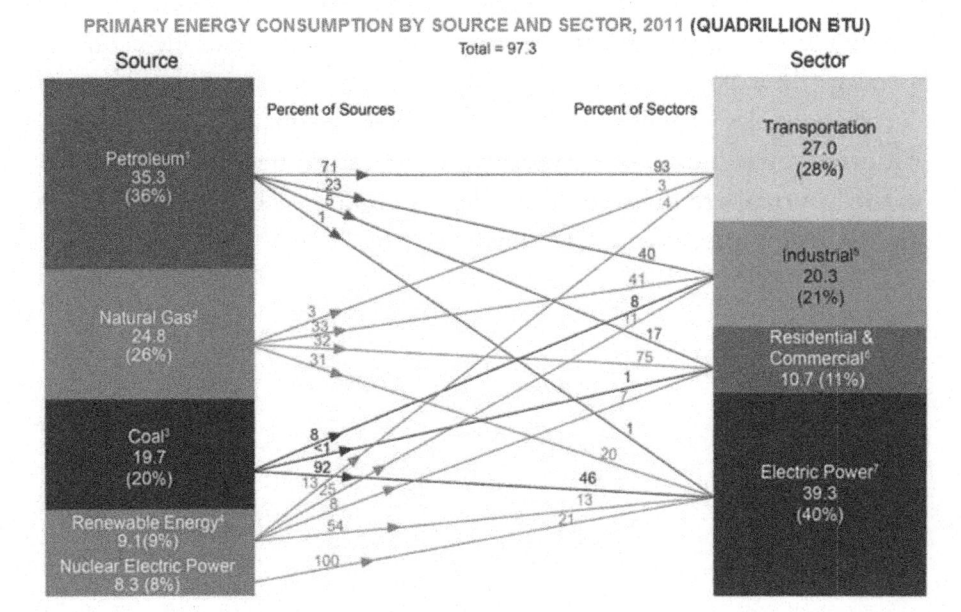

**PRIMARY ENERGY CONSUMPTION BY SOURCE AND SECTOR, 2011 (QUADRILLION BTU)**
Total = 97.3

| Source | Sector |
|---|---|
| Petroleum[1] 35.3 (36%) | Transportation 27.0 (28%) |
| Natural Gas[2] 24.8 (26%) | Industrial[5] 20.3 (21%) |
| Coal[3] 19.7 (20%) | Residential & Commercial[6] 10.7 (11%) |
| Renewable Energy[4] 9.1 (9%) | Electric Power[7] 39.3 (40%) |
| Nuclear Electric Power 8.3 (8%) | |

(Reference: 9.1)

**America has the energy resources to power its economy for hundreds of years, if not forever.** The only issue Americans should be concerned with is assuring America's vast energy resources are developed and used as efficiently as possible. Think about it: America has literally hundreds of years in reserves of oil, natural gas and coal. Additionally, America has areas where solar and wind energy can be harnessed to create electricity. Then there are the extensive lands that can be used to create bio-fuels.

**As previously stated, oil is the cornerstone of America's energy and economic system.** But, oil as well as other fossil fuels, has fallen out of favor due to CO2 emissions which are at the heart of the global warming debate. Americans need to accept the premise CO2 emissions as a result of the use of fossil fuels, is a major cause of global warming. The debate must now focus on identifying a solution for CO2 emissions that will have the least negative impact on the lives of most Americans.

**Oil is more than just energy to fuel America's economy.** Oil is an essential component of many, if not most, products required for modern living. Think about it: If America can reduce the cost of petroleum products, specifically gasoline and diesel, which will reduce the cost of most products consumed by Americans; all Americans will benefit as if they had received a significant raise in pay!

The pros and cons of oil are addressed first followed by different methods of producing oil. Conventional oil is obtained from traditional drilling. This includes on and off shore drilling. Shale oil is acquired from traditional drilling plus horizontal drilling and fracking. Oil shale is rock like material that does not actually contain oil. Oil shale contains a product referred to as kerogen which requires additional processing to become oil. Finally, there is oil developed from CO2. This is a new procedure that has not been developed to the level required for commercial use. That said, retrieving CO2 from the atmosphere and producing synthetic oil is such an important development that it must be brought to the attention of all Americans.

**All current energy options have advantages and disadvantages.** It is important to have an understanding of each energy option before creating an energy policy with maximum benefits for most Americans.

# ENERGY MARKETS AND TRADING

**Prior to discussing individual fuels, there is a situation that has great impact on energy costs for most Americans.** Energy, specifically oil, is traded on the open market as a commodity. What does this mean to most Americans? By allowing energy to be traded as a commodity, the price of energy can be manipulated by investors and speculators. This means the price of energy will often have no correlation with supply and demand. In other words, energy consumers are not only paying for the energy they use but are also required to pay a premium that goes to the investors and speculators.

The obvious response would be for the U.S. to restrict energy buyers to businesses that distribute and/or process energy products. Eliminate speculation that can drive up prices based on nothing more than emotions or world events. But can the U.S. unilaterally change the energy markets? The major commodity market is in the U.S. There is little doubt the U.S. could enact regulations that would prevent energy speculation in America. The problem is that the speculation would likely move to commodity markets outside the control of the U.S.

Additionally, there would be a concern with how the oil producing countries would respond to the U.S. eliminating energy speculators from the energy market. There is a high probability that some, if not all the oil producing countries, would place some restrictions on oil shipments to America. This could likely result in higher fuel prices plus potential fuel shortages for most Americans. But this response from oil producing countries might be good for America. It could accelerate America's efforts to become energy self-sufficient!

## JULY 25, 2013, NATIONAL ASSOCIATION OF CONVENIENCE STORES, (NACS DAILY):

"Oil prices and gas prices are as much about the 'what if.' It's about what could happen. It's a commodity," said Jeff Lenard with NACS.

With supplies pretty much the same as they have been for the past five years, and demand lower, what's driving up gasoline prices? **Speculation.** "And when there's uncertainty, commodities increase in value," he said. "When there's uncertainty in the stock market, prices go down because they're not sure about the company. When there's uncertainty about the commodity, prices go up and that's what we're seeing now, largely because of Egypt." **On Wall Street, hedge fund speculators have snapped up more oil than Oklahoma has sitting in giant oil terminals.**

(Reference: 10.1)

## SHORTLY THEREAFTER, NACS ALSO REPORTED:

August 7, 2013
WASHINGTON – Crude oil prices increased during the first three weeks of July 2013 as world oil markets tightened in the face of seasonal increases in world consumption, unexpected supply disruptions, and heightened uncertainty over the security of supply with the renewed unrest in Egypt.

**Included in the same article**:

The **discount** of West Texas Intermediate (WTI) crude oil to Brent crude oil, which averaged $18 per barrel in 2012 and increased to a monthly average of $21 per barrel in February 2013, closed below $1.50 per barrel on July 19, 2013, and averaged $3 per barrel for the month. The strong demand for light, sweet crude oil in the Midwest and **new pipeline capacity** to deliver production from the West Texas Permian Basin directly to the Gulf Coast contributed to the price of WTI rising relative to Brent crude oil.

(Reference: 10.2)

This is just an example of oil information over a short period of time during 2013. **The end result is that America's energy costs must be insulated from the influence of world events as well as the manipulation of energy prices due to investors and speculators.** This may seem contrary to free enterprise but free enterprise is between manufacturers, resellers and consumers. Free enterprise should not include speculators that do not add value to products and/or services being marketed. Furthermore, Americans should not be expected to suffer economically as a result of events occurring elsewhere in the world.

**A subtle point in the second NACS article is the construction of a pipeline from the West Texas oil fields to the Gulf of Mexico terminals resulting in potentially HIGHER fuel costs for Americans.** Why? Prior to the construction of the pipeline, Middle America had essentially exclusive access to the West Texas oil. After the construction of the pipeline, West Texas oil suddenly had a major new market with a lower delivery cost advantage over imported oil. Rather than the transfer of America's wealth overseas, American energy consumers are now transferring their wealth to oil companies operating within the boundaries of America. Who benefited from the West Texas pipeline? Not the average American consumer!

**The West Texas pipeline highlights an important point related to the marketing of America's energy resources.** America's energy resources may be on private property plus be developed by private and public businesses. Regardless of the location of fossil fuels the disposition of America's energy resources must be regulated in a manner that is in the best interest of most Americans. America's energy resources must be used to enhance the lives of Americans. America's leaders must enact energy policies that ascertain Americans will be able to gain a competitive edge as a result of lower energy prices which will allow the development of products and services by Americans; that are then marketed nationally and internationally.

**There is another issue with imported oil that is really a two edged sword.** When one of the oil producing countries experiences an 'outage', America could be without the oil it needs. An 'outage' can be the result of multiple problems with production and delivery including political unrest. At a minimum, an 'outage' will result in higher prices as they have done in last half of 2013. The chart below shows that unplanned outages in the last half of 2013 are the highest since 2009. The market price during this period reflects the cost of the outage for Americans.

**Estimated Unplanned OPEC Crude Oil Production Outages**
thousand barrels per day

- Iraq
- Nigeria
- Libya
- Iran

(Reference: 10.3)

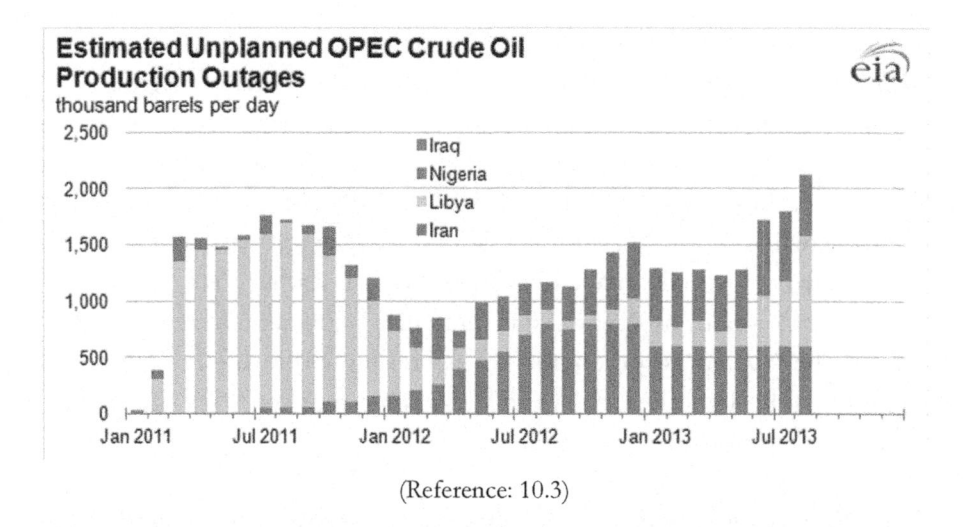

As the 'unplanned OPEC outages' increased, the oil market price increased to more than $110 per barrel. It doesn't matter if America purchases oil from the country experiencing the outage. The overall market price will increase due to World supply and demand. **This is exactly why it is important for America to do whatever is necessary to make sure the price of America's fossil fuels are not influenced by World events or markets.**

**The value of the dollar as compared to other currencies can impact the cost of energy for Americans.** The dollar is the currency which oil prices are determined. If the value of the dollar increases in reference to other currencies there is a potential for oil market prices to decrease. That's good for Americans and not so good for other countries. When the dollar's value decreases in comparison to other currencies, you can bet oil market prices will increase. This is good for other countries but bad for Americans. The cost of oil produced in America must not be influenced by the value of the dollar in comparison to other currencies.

**On October 9, 2013, The Wall Street Journal published an article titled:** *U. S. Refiner Exports Hit High.* The article focused on U. S.

refineries using America's crude oil to produce fuel for export to *'the four corners of the world'*. There is little doubt that the oil producers, refiners, marketers and energy speculators are enjoying significant financial gain from America's emerging energy boom. What about most Americans? How are they benefiting from the increased production of America's oil and natural gas? What about the Federal Law prohibiting, with few exceptions, the export of America's crude oil? Is the oil industry taking advantage of a loop hole in the law? Is the oil industry damaging America's current economy while selling the future of younger Americans? **Unless the American voters unite and make it clear that America's energy resources are to be used to fuel America's economy, the future of America as well as the battle against global warming is lost.**

# OIL, MORE THAN JUST ENERGY

**Products made from a barrel of crude oil, 2012**
gallons

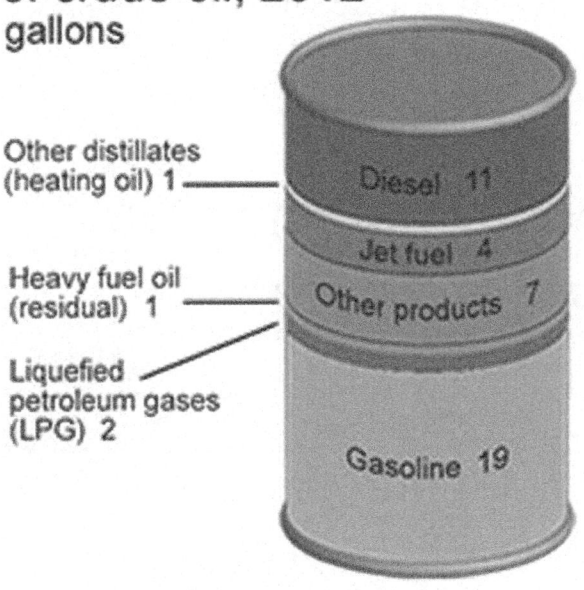

- Other distillates (heating oil) 1
- Heavy fuel oil (residual) 1
- Liquefied petroleum gases (LPG) 2
- Diesel 11
- Jet fuel 4
- Other products 7
- Gasoline 19

(Reference: 11.1)

**According the U.S. Energy Information Agency, (EIA):** *"Petroleum products include transportation fuels, fuel oils for heating and electricity generation, asphalt and road oil, and the feedstocks used to make chemicals, plastics, and synthetic materials found in nearly everything we use today."* **Think about it, there is no way life, as Americans know it, can continue without oil.**

The list of products derived from oil is extensive but the following is a partial list of the most common.

| | | | |
|---|---|---|---|
| Anesthetics | Detergents | Ice Cube Trays | Safety Glasses |
| Ammonia | Diesel fuel | Ink | Shag Rugs |
| Antifreeze | Dishes | Insect Repellent | Shampoo |
| Antihistamines | Dresses | Insecticides | Shaving Cream |
| Antiseptics | Drinking Cups | Life Jackets | Shoe Polish |
| Artificial limbs | Dyes | Linings | Shoes |
| Aspirin | Electric Blankets | Linoleum | Shower Curtains |
| Awnings | Electrician's Tape | Lipstick | Skis |
| Balloons | Enamel | Luggage | Slacks |
| Ballpoint Pens | Epoxy | Model Cars | Soap |
| Bandages | Eyeglasses | Mops | Soft Contact lenses |
| Basketballs | Fan Belts | Motor Oil | Solvents |
| Bicycle Tires | Fertilizers | Motorcycle Helmet | Speakers |
| Boats | Fishing Boots | Nail Polish | Sun Glasses |
| Cameras | Fishing lures | Nylon Rope | Surf Boards |
| Candles | Fishing Rods | Oil Filters | Sweaters |
| Car Battery Cases | Floor Wax | Paint | Synthetic Rubber |
| Car Enamel | Folding Doors | Paint Brushes | Telephones |
| Cassettes | Food Preservatives | Paint Rollers | Tennis Rackets |
| Caulking | Football Cleats | Panty Hose | Tents |
| CD Player | Footballs | Parachutes | Tires |
| CD's & DVD's | Gasoline | Perfumes | Toilet Seats |
| Clothes | Glycerin | Petroleum Jelly | Tool Boxes |
| Clothesline | Golf Bags | Pillows | Tool Racks |
| Cold cream | Golf Balls | Plastic Wood | Toothpaste |
| Combs | Grease | Purses | Transparent Tape |
| Cortisone | Guitar Strings | Putty | Trash Bags |
| Crayons | Hair Coloring | Refrigerant | TV Cabinets |
| Curtains | Hair Curlers | Refrigerators | Umbrellas |

| Dashboards | Hand Lotion | Roller Skates | Upholstery |
| Denture Adhesive | Heart Valves | Roofing | Vaporizers |
| Dentures | House Paint | Rubber Cement | Vitamin Capsules |
| Deodorant | Ice Chests | Rubbing Alcohol | Water Pipes |

(Reference: 11.2)

**Clearly, oil is and will continue to be the cornerstone of modern life, a reality that cannot be denied.** The fact that America's elected leaders have allowed oil required for our very existence to be controlled by foreign governments, investors and speculators is intolerable and cannot continue. Everything else aside, it should be clear that America needs a secure, reliable and affordable source of oil for now and the foreseeable future. **If America's elected leaders do not develop all of America's oil resources, they are either incompetent, guilty of reckless leadership or even treason; and clearly endangering the future of most Americans.**

Does this mean America is to ignore global warming as a result of $CO_2$ emissions emitted by the use of fossil fuels and other human activity? Absolutely not! At the same time Americans must accept the fact that oil and other fossil fuels are essential for the continued existence of American society as well as the survival of all mankind. **Additionally, simply reducing the consumption of fossil fuels will not halt global warming.** As stated multiple times, the current levels of atmospheric $CO_2$ are more than adequate to create temperatures unacceptable for the human race.

**America must use the economic power it creates from sustained use of fossil fuels to develop the technology required to monitor and control atmospheric $CO_2$. Unless America assumes the responsibility for this effort, it is extremely unlikely global warming can be stopped.**

# THE LONG TERM IMPACT OF REFINERY EXPORTS?

**How much of an impact on retail gasoline prices does the price of crude oil have?** The cost per barrel of crude oil represents approximately two thirds of the retail price of gasoline. A barrel of crude oil contains 42 gallons and will produce approximately 19 gallons of gasoline. Every dollar increase in the cost of a barrel of crude oil will require an increase of approximately 2.4 cents per gallon increase in the wholesale cost of gasoline, [Price Increase = ((19/42)/19) = .0238 or approximately 2.4 cents]. Since the cost of oil represents approximately 67% of the price of gasoline, (67% = .67 numerically); the retail price for a gallon of gasoline will likely increase by approximately 3.6 cents per gallon due to other costs and profits. (Total retail price increase for $1.00 increase in the cost of a barrel of crude oil = (.0238/.67) = .0355 or approximately 3.6 cents) Obviously, a dollar reduction in the cost of a barrel of crude oil will decrease the wholesale cost and retail price of gasoline by the same amount.

**No other consumer product has a greater impact on the economic confidence of Americans than the retail price of gasoline.** An unfortunate situation since the retail price of diesel has a far greater impact on most Americans' cost of living than gasoline prices. Virtually everything purchased by Americans have been distributed by trucks and trains which operate on diesel. If all things are equal, which they are not, a dollar change in the cost of a barrel of oil should impact the wholesale price of diesel by 2.4 cents per gallon. The refining costs for gasoline and diesel are not the same but more importantly, there is an even bigger influence on the price of diesel. American refiners are exporting increasing amounts of diesel to markets outside the United States. Due to the fact a barrel of crude oil produces limited amounts of gasoline, diesel and other products; America is benefiting from lower gasoline prices due to America's refineries producing more gasoline than the American market can consume as a result of demand for diesel by other countries. This results in lower gasoline prices for most Americans.

Should America continue to increase diesel exports to further reduce gasoline prices in America? Sounds like a good idea: Additional decreases in gasoline prices will make Americans more confident and willing to spend more on other products creating an overall economic boost. Clearly, America needs to increase diesel exports. Not so fast! Americans need to look beyond today.

**If America is to develop and sustain the strong economy required for America to deal with global climate change, America cannot allow America's energy costs to be influenced by events outside America.** Clearly, the increasing export of diesel is influencing the price Americans pay for gasoline; as well as the transportation costs for other products Americans purchase. Americans must not allow long term objectives to be derailed by short term benefits. Rest assured, the current benefit of lower gasoline prices, as a result of increased diesel exports, will end. What prevents refiners from exporting gasoline? What will happen to America's fuel prices if the extra gasoline production is exported with the diesel?

**America needs the refinery capacity required to produce the fuel and products necessary for Americans to create, sustain and protect an economy providing the jobs and opportunities most Americans desire and expect.** Since crude oil and natural gas are America's primary energy resources as well as essential ingredients for virtually every consumer product; Americans need to make sure no new or existing laws or regulations will prevent America from maintaining the refinery capacity required to meet America's energy and economic needs. The primary objective of America's refineries should be the processing of American crude oil and natural gas to supply America's economy. Excess refinery capacity should be allowed to produce products for export but only from crude oil and natural gas imported for that purpose. In other words, America's natural energy resources must be used exclusively to fuel America's economy.

# CONVENTIONAL OIL

***Okemah, OK 1922 Gusher Photo***

(Reference: 13.1)

Oil produced from traditional oil well drilling, including offshore wells, is classified as conventional oil for the purposes of this book. Conventional oil is the easiest oil to locate and produce. The 'gusher' pictured above was a relatively common occurrence early on in the development of oil wells. Today, conventional oil sometimes requires innovative technology to be forced to the surface. Many of America's oil fields have been in production for decades and due to advances in oil production technology are still producing oil well beyond their forecasted life expectancy. This fact is a tribute to America's capitalistic economy which encourages and rewards ingenuity!

## SECURE OUR SHIP! FUEL AMERICA NOW!

Source: U.S. Energy Information Administration
**U.S. Crude Oil Proved Reserves (Million Barrels)**

| Decade | Year-0 | Year-1 | Year-2 | Year-3 | Year-4 | Year-5 | Year-6 | Year-7 | Year-8 | Year-9 |
|---|---|---|---|---|---|---|---|---|---|---|
| 1970's | 39,001 | 38,063 | 36,339 | 35,300 | 32,250 | 32,682 | 30,942 | 31,780 | 31,355 | 29,810 |
| 1980's | 29,805 | 29,426 | 27,858 | 27,735 | 28,446 | 28,416 | 26,889 | 27,256 | 26,825 | 26,501 |
| 1990's | 26,254 | 24,682 | 23,745 | 22,957 | 22,457 | 22,351 | 22,017 | 22,546 | 21,034 | 21,765 |
| 2000's | 22,045 | 22,446 | 22,677 | 21,891 | 21,371 | 21,757 | 20,972 | 21,317 | 19,121 | 20,682 |
| 2010's | 23,267 | | | | | | | | | |

(Reference: 13.2)

America's official crude oil reserves are based on conventional oil. Unconventional oil, which is dealt with separately in this book, is not included in America's official oil reserves. America's conventional oil reserves peaked in 1970 and decreased until 2008. Since 2008 America's projected oil reserves have increased due to advances in oil well drilling technology. The most important technological advances are referred to as horizontal drilling plus fracturing or fracking. Fracking has been the most controversial. At the time of the writing of this book, there has been no environmental damage that can be linked to fracking. But, if at some future time, fracking is linked to environmental damage, the fracking situation must be evaluated and corrective action taken. It is important that logic supersede emotion. Without fracking, a large portion of America's oil reserves will no longer be available.

Currently, America consumes slightly less than 7 billion barrels of oil per year. Based on that rate of consumption, America has approximately 3 to 4 years of proven conventional oil reserves. Americans should not be overly concerned about America's official oil reserves. America's annual oil consumption has ranged between 5.8 billion and nearly 7.6 billion barrels of oil for more than 30 years. During the same period America's estimated oil reserves have remained between 19 to 29 billion barrels.

## CONVENTIONAL OIL

Source: U.S. Energy Information Administration

**U.S. Product Supplied of Crude Oil and Petroleum Products (Thousand Barrels)**

| Decade | Year-0 | Year-1 | Year-2 | Year-3 | Year-4 | Year-5 | Year-6 | Year-7 | Year-8 | Year-9 |
|---|---|---|---|---|---|---|---|---|---|---|
| 1980's |  | 5,861,058 | 5,582,938 | 5,559,364 | 5,755,575 | 5,740,143 | 5,942,429 | 6,082,742 | 6,325,692 | 6,323,681 |
| 1990's | 6,200,801 | 6,100,550 | 6,234,025 | 6,291,407 | 6,467,128 | 6,469,475 | 6,701,059 | 6,796,411 | 6,904,756 | 7,124,558 |
| 2000's | 7,210,594 | 7,171,777 | 7,212,876 | 7,312,229 | 7,587,601 | 7,592,789 | 7,550,908 | 7,548,338 | 7,136,255 | 6,851,561 |
| 2010's | 7,000,746 | 6,916,552 | 6,790,973 |  |  |  |  |  |  |  |

(Reference: 13.3)

Advances in oil well technology with offshore drilling occurring in deeper and deeper waters, America's conventional oil reserves should remain in the 20 billion barrel range or higher. With technological advances allowing for more efficient use of oil derived fuels along with America's floundering economy, conventional oil consumption should be reduced substantially, creating even higher oil reserve forecasts.

Imported oil to fuel America's economy must be eliminated or at a minimum, become insignificant. Oil imported to be refined with the derived fuel and products being exported will create jobs and opportunities for Americans. The additional refinery capacity used for refining foreign oil should also be available to sustain America's need for energy in the event a refinery is temporarily shut down for maintenance or seasonal adjustments to production.

As America ends its dependence on imported oil, the consumption of America's conventional oil resources will increase. The increasing consumption of America's conventional oil resources could be more rapid than the gains in forecasted reserves. If America is to successfully reduce its reliance on oil imports, America will need to develop its unconventional oil resources.

## U.S. Crude Oil and Liquid Fuels Supply, Consumption, and Inventories

Source: U. S. Energy Information Agency, (EIA.gov)

Millions of Barrels per Day

| | 2008 | 2009 | 2010 | 2011 | 2012 | 2013 | 2014 |
|---|---|---|---|---|---|---|---|
| **Supply** | | | | | | | |
| **Crude Oil Supply** | | | | | | | |
| Domestic Production [a] | 5.00 | 5.35 | 5.48 | 5.65 | 6.50 | 7.31 | 8.09 |
| Alaska | 0.68 | 0.65 | 0.60 | 0.56 | 0.53 | 0.50 | 0.47 |
| Federal Gulf of Mexico [b] | 1.16 | 1.56 | 1.55 | 1.32 | 1.27 | 1.26 | 1.39 |
| Other Lower 48 States (excl. GOM) | 3.16 | 3.15 | 3.33 | 3.77 | 4.70 | 5.55 | 6.22 |
| Crude Oil Net Imports [c] | 9.75 | 8.97 | 9.17 | 8.89 | 8.43 | 7.52 | 6.85 |
| SPR Net Withdrawals | -0.01 | -0.07 | 0.00 | 0.08 | 0.00 | 0.00 | 0.00 |
| Commercial Inventory Net Withdrawals | -0.11 | 0.00 | -0.02 | 0.01 | -0.09 | 0.01 | -0.02 |
| Crude Oil Adjustment [d] | 0.02 | 0.08 | 0.10 | 0.17 | 0.17 | 0.19 | 0.18 |
| Total Crude Oil Input to Refineries | 14.65 | 14.34 | 14.72 | 14.81 | 15.01 | 15.03 | 15.09 |

a  Includes lease condensate.
b  Crude oil production from U.S. Federal leases in the Gulf of Mexico (GOM).
c  Net imports equals gross imports minus gross exports.
d  Crude oil adjustment balances supply and consumption and was previously referred to as "Unaccounted for Crude Oil."

(Reference: 13.4)

According to U.S. Energy Information Agency, (EIA), the week ending May 31, 2013, U.S. oil production exceeded imports for the first time since January, 1997. The EIA also projects the U.S. oil production should exceed oil imports for the entire year of 2014. America is moving in the right direction in reducing oil imports but without developing America's vast unconventional oil resources it is extremely unlikely America can eliminate oil imports. Solar, wind, nuclear, bio-fuels plus other renewable and/or green energies can reduce oil consumption but these energy resources cannot replace oil.

## CONVENTIONAL OIL

**Conventional Oil Production - Imports**

Conventional Oil = Oil pumped from drilled wells.

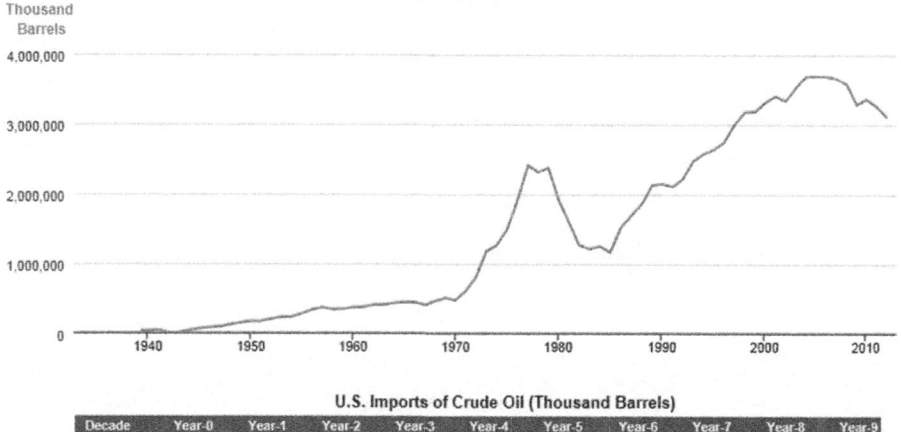

**U.S. Imports of Crude Oil (Thousand Barrels)**

| Decade | Year-0 | Year-1 | Year-2 | Year-3 | Year-4 | Year-5 | Year-6 | Year-7 | Year-8 | Year-9 |
|---|---|---|---|---|---|---|---|---|---|---|
| 1940's | 42,662 | 50,606 | 12,297 | 13,833 | 44,815 | 74,337 | 86,066 | 97,532 | 129,093 | 153,686 |
| 1950's | 177,714 | 179,073 | 209,591 | 236,455 | 239,479 | 285,421 | 341,833 | 373,255 | 348,007 | 352,344 |
| 1960's | 371,575 | 381,548 | 411,039 | 412,660 | 438,643 | 452,040 | 447,120 | 411,649 | 472,323 | 514,114 |
| 1970's | 483,293 | 613,417 | 811,135 | 1,183,996 | 1,269,155 | 1,498,181 | 1,935,012 | 2,414,327 | 2,319,826 | 2,379,541 |
| 1980's | 1,926,162 | 1,604,703 | 1,273,214 | 1,215,225 | 1,253,949 | 1,168,297 | 1,524,978 | 1,705,922 | 1,869,005 | 2,132,761 |
| 1990's | 2,151,387 | 2,110,532 | 2,226,341 | 2,477,230 | 2,578,072 | 2,638,810 | 2,747,839 | 3,002,299 | 3,177,584 | 3,186,663 |
| 2000's | 3,319,816 | 3,404,894 | 3,336,175 | 3,527,696 | 3,692,063 | 3,695,971 | 3,693,081 | 3,661,404 | 3,580,694 | 3,289,675 |
| 2010's | 3,362,856 | 3,261,422 | 3,107,825 | | | | | | | |

Source: U.S. Energy Information Agency, (EIA)

(Reference: 13.5)

The chart and table above provide insight into America's oil imports since 1940 through 2012. Note that in 1977 America's oil imports began to decrease until 1983. After 1983 oil imports increased until 2010 when the oil imports began another decreasing trend. Two questions need to be asked: Why are oil imports decreasing? How long will oil imports continue to decrease?

The answer to the first question is: Oil imports are shrinking due to escalating oil costs which reduce demand plus technological advances in oil and natural gas production that have significantly increased America's oil and natural gas production. Also, wind, solar and bio-fuels have contributed to the reduction in America's oil imports.

How long will oil imports continue to decrease? If America continues to limit oil production to conventional sources, regardless of advances in technology and conservation, at some point in the near future, America will once again be forced to increase oil imports. **If America is to become energy independent, America must develop all its energy resources, specifically non-conventional oil.**

How did America become dependent on foreign oil? Shortly after World War 2, (WWII), America became a net oil importer. President Truman acknowledged the importance of oil by appointing the Paley Commission to study the security of America's oil supply. The commission supported policies for greater domestic production, particularly from oil shale. Unfortunately, the commission advised against increasing trade barriers on imported oil. As a result of the availability of low cost foreign oil, imports increased in spite of concerns for America's energy security. In 1958, President Eisenhower imposed quotas that limited imports east of the Rockies, which due to loopholes and rising oil prices broke down by 1969. President Nixon replaced the program with an import fee in 1974 of only a few cents per barrel of oil. The groundwork was now complete for America to sacrifice its energy security for low cost oil. **As a result of politics not in the best interest of America, most Americans continue to struggle with increasing and unpredictable energy costs.**

# SHALE OIL

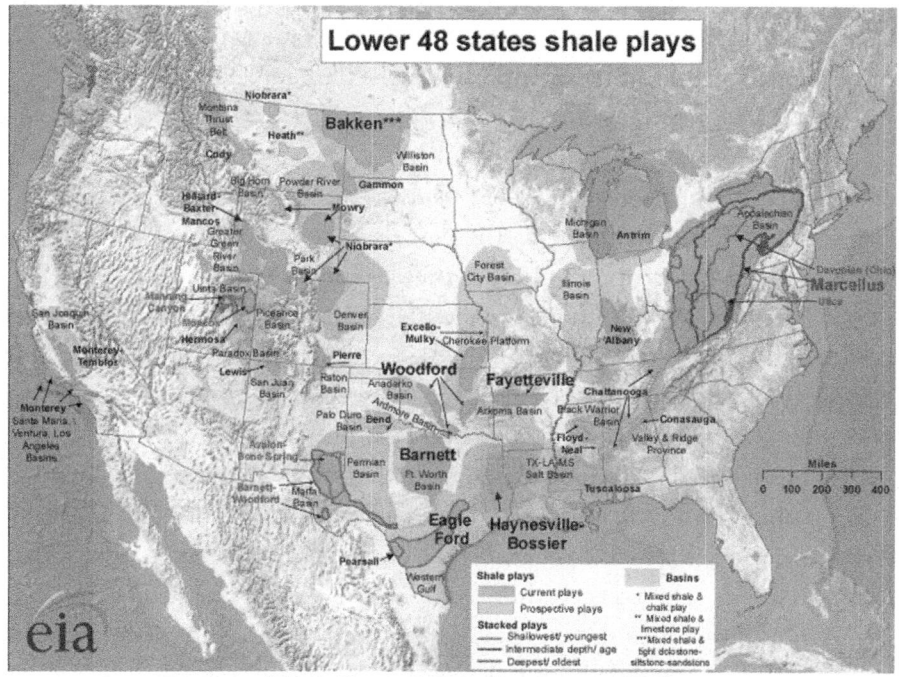

Courtesy of: U. S. Energy Information Agency, (EIA)

(Reference: 14.1)

Americans might believe America's shale oil reserves are recent discoveries. The fact is most, if not all, shale oil deposits have been common knowledge within the oil industry for decades. The problem has been the technology required to profitably produce oil and/or natural gas from shale has not been available.

Distorted facts and half truths presented by public media along with Hollywood propaganda films, many Americans may believe fracking is a new process that should be discontinued due to the potential to contaminate ground water. Believe it or not, fracking was first used in the oil industry in 1947 with the first commercial application in 1949. Also, as much as 60% of new oil and natural gas wells involve fracking. The actual fracking process will likely occur thousands of feet below most ground water. In the event there is contamination, the fault will likely be due to improper oil well drilling, most likely the well casing. The actual fracking process has a low probability of contaminating ground water.

If water contamination does occur, the cause needs to be identified and corrective action taken. Due to the fact that oil drilling has been around for more than a century and before the development of adequate oil well drilling regulations, there is a substantial probability that older oil wells could contaminate ground water. These wells should be identified and as necessary, corrective action undertaken. Newer oil wells were likely drilled under the guidance of federal and state environmental regulatory agencies and subject to regulations devised to reduce the probability of ground water contamination. Violation of the regulations will result in substantial fines. In the event a newer oil well is the cause of ground water contamination and was developed according to the regulations in effect at the time of drilling, additional regulations may be required to prevent reoccurrence of the problem. Oil well drilling must continue due to the fact that America needs oil. Reason must prevail over emotions.

The technology that really made shale oil a commercial resource is fracking combined with horizontal drilling. Early fracking occurred in vertically drilled oil wells that passed through tight formations containing oil and/or natural gas. Since the strata containing the oil and/or natural gas could be just a few feet thick, the fracking would have marginal returns. Once horizontal drilling was developed, the well could be drilled down to the oil/natural gas strata and then follow the strata for thousands of feet. Fracking is far more effective when it can be applied in more and more oil/natural gas bearing material.

## SHALE OIL

The fact is: Without shale oil produced as result of horizontal drilling plus fracking, America will have a far more difficult time achieving energy independence.

# OIL SHALE

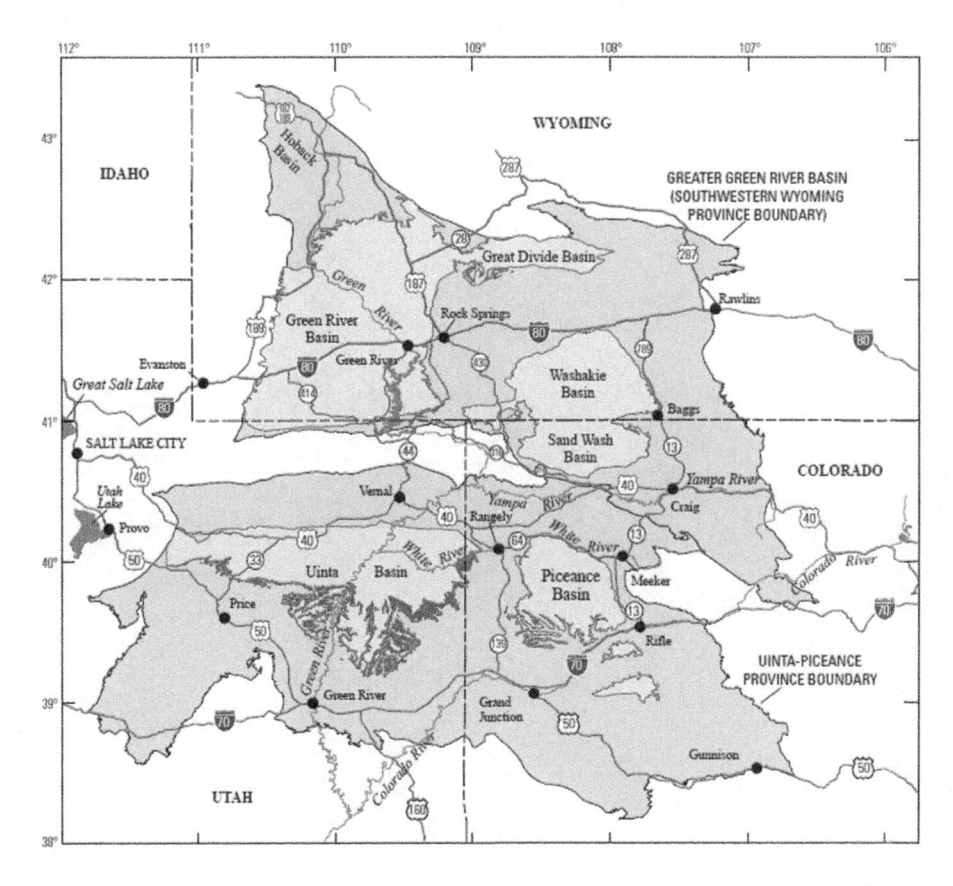

(Reference: 15.1)

Oil shale is America's 'Ace in the hole'! There is more oil, (actually a product called kerogen which is not fully formed oil), contained in America's oil shale than accessible in any other country in the world including Saudi Arabia! No one knows for sure how much oil could be produced from America's oil shale. The amount oil that could be produced from America's oil shale may well be in the trillions of barrels. How long would a trillion barrels of oil last America? America could easily have several centuries of oil reserves contained in its oil shale.

## OIL SHALE

Oil shale's importance to America's energy security is not a new idea. As stated in a previous section, after WWII, President Truman appointed a special commission to study America's oil requirements and supply sources. The commission recommended that America's oil shale be developed as a secure source of oil.

America's oil shale could be vital to America's energy independence and security. But America' oil shale is classified as unconventional oil. This means the oil is not in a form that can be easily produced using conventional drilling and pumping. Oil obtained from oil shale is significantly more expensive to produce than drilling and pumping conventional oil. Production of oil shale will require significant quantities of water and energy. As most Americans realize, water in the western U. S. is not readily available and all available water coveted by farmers, ranchers, businesses and cities.

What should be important to most Americans is that the vast majority of oil shale, (75% or more), is located on public lands, including the areas of oil shale considered the most productive. What does this mean for Americans? The government would be entitled to oil royalties that would otherwise be paid to private land owners. This could provide a significant revenue stream that could be used to pay down America's debt and/or fund the development of technology to reverse climate change. Americans must make sure that special interest groups do not manipulate government officials into reducing or even eliminating the royalties that could be generated from development of America's oil shale.

If oil shale has the potential of eliminating America's dependence on foreign oil, why has it not been developed? First, efforts have and are being made to develop America's oil shale. In the early 1900's oil shale was too expensive to develop due to the low cost and readily available conventional oil. In the 1970's and early 1980's, the oil industry did undertake a significant effort to produce oil from oil shale. OPEC's oil embargo resulting in inadequate oil supplies plus rapidly increasing oil prices had made oil shale a commercially viable option. Total investments, likely exceeding five billion dollars were made in an effort to develop America's oil shale. Then on May 2, 1982, as a result of rapidly decreasing oil prices, Exxon terminated its oil shale project. More than 2,000 employees were immediately unemployed. The date is referred to by locals as 'Black Sunday'.

Black Sunday is just another example of the influence and control foreign countries have on America's economy and future. OPEC 'opened the taps' and let the oil flow and dropped the price of oil. The management of oil companies is responsible for generating profits and value for shareholders. The logical option at the time was to discontinue the oil shale development effort due to imported oil's cost being less than oil produced from oil shale. As time would prove, that was an extremely short sighted decision. If America had aggressively pursued the development of the oil shale, it is highly probable oil production would be comparable to Canada's oil sands production now nearing 2 million barrels per day.

What if America's elected leaders had set a minimum price for a barrel of oil? In the event world oil prices fell below the minimum price, there would be a tariff that would increase the price of imported oil to the minimum price. Without a doubt the decision would have been controversial at the time but looking back, it could have prevented America from becoming dependent on foreign oil. Also, energy prices in America would have never reached the $147.02 per oil barrel attained on July 11, 2008. By the way, a barrel of oil is 42 gallons, considerably less than the traditional 55 gallon barrel.

# OIL SHALE

The U. S. Department of Energy estimates the production cost of oil shale would range between $35 and $54 per barrel depending on the production method including a 15% profit margin. The International Energy Agency estimates the oil shale production costs would be similar to the Canadian Oil Sands which is in the $60 per barrel range. In 2005, Shell Oil estimated oil shale production costs at $30 per barrel. The important point is oil shale can produce the oil America needs at costs far below current and future international market prices.

Unfortunately, America's oil shale will not be developed without a significant change in American politics. Environmentalists aggressively oppose the development of oil shale on a variety of reasons. Among these blocks to oil shale development are: (1) Global warming emissions from production to consumption of fossil fuels. (2) Alleged environmental damage from the material remaining after the oil has been removed. (3) Potential pollution of ground water. (4) Disruption of wildlife. The list continues but there are no insurmountable reasons America's oil shale should not be developed. As far as environmental damage and wildlife disruption goes, the development of America's oil shale will have far less of an impact than the wind generator and solar energy farms actively promoted by environmentalists. The global warming issue is covered in other sections of this book.

The groundwater issue does have validity due to the fact the oil shale is near the surface rather than deep below the water table. Shell Oil has developed a process of extracting oil from oil shale referred to as 'in situ'. This process heats the shale in place to the point the Kerogen, (a not fully formed oil), which is then pumped similar to pumping conventional oil. To prevent the ground water from being contaminated, Shell creates a 'freeze wall' surrounding the kerogen.

Shell Oil In-situ Facility, Piceance Basin near Rifle, Colorado

(Reference: 15.2)

The other method of producing oil from oil shale is called ex situ. This process is similar to mining coal with the oil shale being processed above ground. The major issue with ex situ is that the material remaining after the extraction of the kerogen is of greater volume than the oil shale that was mined. This is due to the fact that the shale has been finely ground. This just makes the reclamation of the area being mined somewhat more difficult.

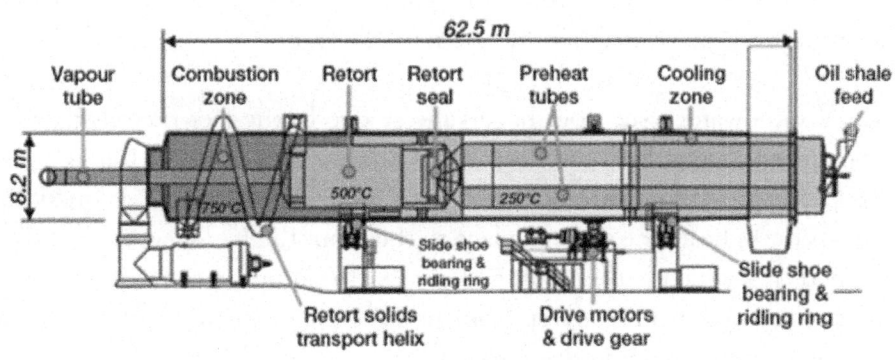

**Courtesy: US Department of Energy - Oil Shale ex situ retorting system.**

(Reference: 15.3)

An advantage of oil shale is the fact that if a processing facility is built to produce 100,000 barrels of oil per day; 100,000 barrels of oil will remain the production rate throughout the life of the facility. Whereas when a new oil well is drilled, the production will be greatest when the well is new. Production will continue to decrease as the well ages.

**Oil shale photograph**

(Reference: 15.4)

# CO$_2$ OIL

How is oil created? Vegetation absorbs CO2 from the atmosphere, releasing the oxygen back into the atmosphere and using carbon to grow. Other living organisms obtain carbon from grazing on vegetation or consuming other living organisms. Once the vegetation and other life forms die and then buried for millions of years under significant pressure; the carbon morphs into different forms of fossil fuels.

What if mankind could not only simulate nature's process of creating oil but rather than require millions of years to complete the process, convert CO2 into oil in a virtually instantaneous process? What would that mean to mankind? The list of benefits for mankind would include: (1) By removing CO2 from the atmosphere, global warming could be controlled. (2) Oil becomes a renewable resource. (3) Every country in the world would have unlimited access to energy. The losers would be the oil producing countries and possibly oil companies.

Is converting CO2 from the atmosphere a possibility or fantasy? Converting CO2 to oil is a reality. The following was taken from Scientific American:

## CO₂ OIL

In the 1990s a graduate student named Lin Chao at Princeton University decided to bubble carbon dioxide into an electrochemical cell. Using cathodes made from the element palladium and a catalyst known as pyridinium—a garden variety organic chemical that is a by-product of oil refining—he discovered that applying an electric current would assemble methanol from the CO2. He published his findings in 1994—and no one cared.

But by 2003, Chao's successor in the Princeton lab of chemist Andrew Bocarsly was deeply interested in finding a solution to the growing problem of the CO2 pollution causing global climate change. Graduate student Emily Barton picked up where he left off and, using an electrochemical cell that employs a semiconducting material used in photovoltaic solar cells for one of its electrodes, succeeded in tapping sunlight to transform CO2 into the basic fuel.

"The dominant thinking 10 years ago was that we should bury the CO2. But if you could efficiently convert it into something that we wouldn't have to spend all that money and energy to put into the ground, sort of recycle it, that would be better," Bocarsly says. "We take CO2, water, sunlight and an appropriate catalyst and generate an alcoholic fuel."

He adds: "We didn't have some brilliant insight here. We had some luck."

**REPRINTED FROM SCIENTIFIC AMERICAN ARTICLE DATED: 9-23-2010**

(Reference: 16.1)

Today, processes to make oil from atmospheric CO2 are being developed by researchers at some of America's major universities as well as in private research laboratories. The issue is that just creating oil from CO2 is just cycling the CO2 between the atmosphere and consumption. Nothing is being done about the excessive CO2 currently in the atmosphere. (If the synthetic oil produced from CO2 can be used in the production of products other than energy, that portion will then be sequestered, much like if the CO2 had been buried.) It may be necessary for governmental regulations to be created to require the sequestering of a certain percentage of the atmospheric CO2 captured in the oil production process. The government would monitor the atmosphere and revise sequestering percentages as necessary.

Since there is an opportunity for unimaginable profits, little, if any investment of public money will be required to develop, implement and operate CO2 to oil conversion facilities. There should be no misappropriation of public funds similar to Solyndra failure in 2011.

Here is an example of CO2 to oil research. According to a USC, (University of Southern California), methanol research project, directed by Nobel Laureate Professor George A. Olah, CO2 can be directly converted into methanol. Initially, the CO2 emissions from power plants could be captured and converted to methanol. The next step would be to capture the CO2 directly from the atmosphere. Think about it, now the CO2 in the atmosphere could actually be reduced plus create a synthetic fossil fuel! Also, the CO2 is free! Not only can methanol fuel conventionally powered automobiles, it can also be used to produce a diesel substitute. Plus, methanol can be easily converted to ethylene and propylene which is used in the petrochemical industry. Lastly, and most importantly, methanol is now a renewable energy resource!

USC is not alone in its research for converting CO2 into a useable energy resource. Other universities and organizations are actively researching methods of converting CO2. The Sandia National Laboratories is working on converting CO2 and water to carbon monoxide, hydrogen and oxygen. Carbon monoxide and hydrogen can be used to produce synthetic fuels. The process requires significant energy which can be provided by the sun.

Sandia National Laboratories refers to the process as 'sunshine to petrol'. Just a few years ago, converting CO2 to energy was virtually unheard of. It will not be long before some organization is profitably converting CO2 to a synthetic petroleum product. What does this mean? **Maybe, oil, all-be-it synthetically derived, is the energy of the future!**

It would be great if the CO2 to oil technology was ready for commercial production. Regrettably, that is not the case. America will have to rely on other sources of energy until CO2 to oil is a reality. But, it is of utmost importance the technology required to remove CO2 from the atmosphere being developed and implemented as quickly as possible. Until it is possible to extract large quantities of CO2 from the atmosphere, there is no possibility of eliminating the global warming threat. If the extracted CO2 can be converted to oil, the motivation to develop and apply the required technology is increased significantly.

It is important to emphasize the fact that removing CO2 from the atmosphere and creating oil or other fossil fuels does not reduce the atmospheric CO2 levels. That is due to the fact that as soon as the oil or other fossil fuel is consumed, the CO2 which was converted is returned to the atmosphere. If the atmospheric CO2 is too high, the CO2 removed will have to be sequestered, (stored), in a manner that prevents its return to the atmosphere. The CO2 conversion to fossil fuels will only be feasible when the atmospheric CO2 levels are where they need to be to end global warming. Due to the imbalance in the amount of carbon being emitted into the atmosphere significantly exceeding the CO2 being removed from the atmosphere by plants, trees and other CO2 sinks, there will always be a need to artificially remove excess atmospheric CO2. The excess CO2 will need to be sequestered. (As previously stated the CO2 sequestration may take the form of non-energy products developed from the CO2 derived synthetic oil.)

# COAL

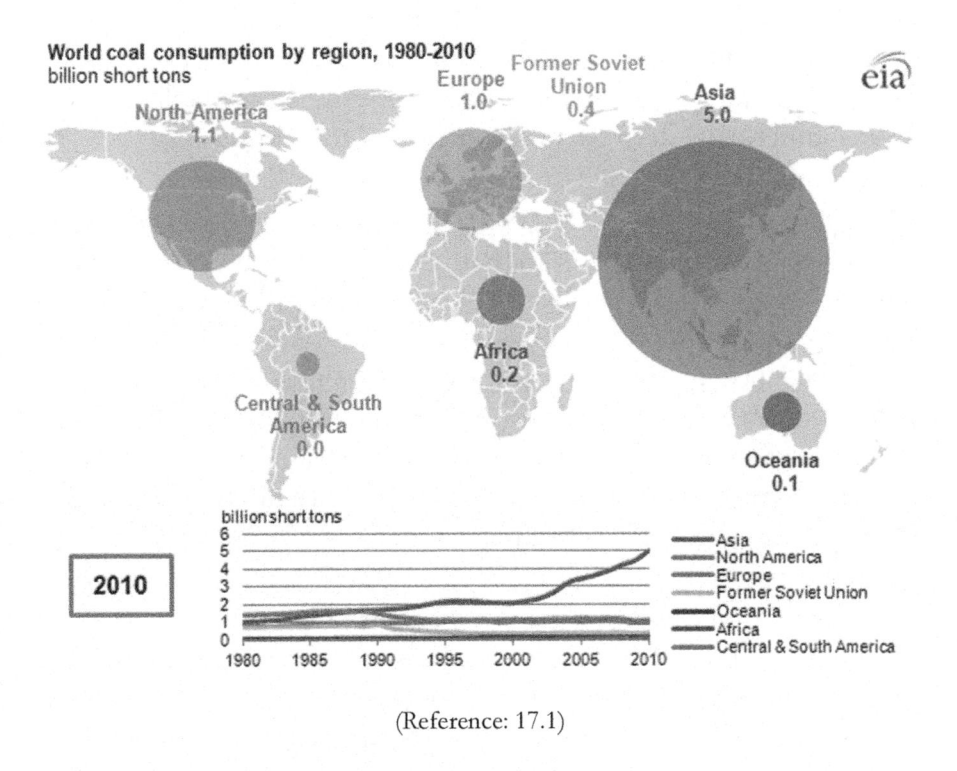

**World coal consumption by region, 1980-2010**
billion short tons

- North America 1.1
- Europe 1.0
- Former Soviet Union 0.4
- Asia 5.0
- Africa 0.2
- Central & South America 0.0
- Oceania 0.1

2010

(Reference: 17.1)

Coal is used worldwide, primarily for the generation of electricity but also used as an energy source for some manufacturers. As the figure above clearly shows, Asia consumes more coal than the remainder of the world. Also, according to the graph within the figure above, the use of coal is increasing rapidly within the Asian region. What effect will this increasing use of coal have on $CO_2$ emissions?

The key objection for the use of coal is its relatively high $CO_2$ emissions per BTU, (British Thermal Unit, a standard measure of heat generated). Coal's upside is the fact that America has literally hundreds of years in coal reserves. Additionally, coal's primary use is to fuel power plants which generate electricity. Since electricity generated with coal is produced by stationary power plants, coal's $CO_2$ emissions that traditionally were emitted into the atmosphere can be captured and sequestered. (At some point, when the required technology is available, the $CO_2$ produced by burning coal can be converted into synthetic oil.)

There is a consortium of government and industry implementing the technology required to capture and sequester 90% of coal's $CO_2$ emissions. The construction of this project began in 2013 and is expected to be completed in 2017. The project is referred to as FutureGen and is being implemented in Meredosia, IL. This is an interesting location since President Obama is from Illinois and during President Obama's first campaign for president he said: *"If somebody wants to build a coal-powered plant, they can, it's just that it will bankrupt them."* In 2013, President Obama appears to be rethinking his original position since he is allowing a nearly 2 billion dollar project for the development of technology to sequester $CO_2$ emitted by a coal burning power plant that could give new life to the coal industry. Apparently, once President Obama evaluated America's real life energy situation, he decided it might be advantageous to hedge his bet.

Another important event stressing the importance of coal for America is a statement made by the U. S. Secretary of Energy, Ernest Moniz: *"No discussion of U.S. energy security and reducing global $CO_2$ emissions is complete without talking about coal—and the technologies that will allow us to use this resource more efficiently and with fewer greenhouse gas emissions."* Clearly, coal does have a future in America. Additionally, coal use worldwide is the fastest growing energy resource among the fossil fuels.

The next step might be not be to sequester all the $CO_2$ emitted from the burning of coal but to process the $CO_2$ to produce synthetic oil. Not only could this be a new source of oil but the revenue generated could reduce the overall cost of the electricity being generated.

With America having access to a virtually unlimited supply of coal along with fact that coal's CO2 emissions can be captured rather than being released into the atmosphere, coal should remain a significant fuel for the generation of electricity. Also, it is possible to convert coal to oil. South Africa has been converting coal to oil since 1955 with a plant producing in excess of 160,000 barrels of oil per day. Other countries with significant coal supplies are in various stages of creating oil from coal. This is just another option for America to attain energy independence.

The University of Texas in Arlington, Texas, announced in 2010 that a new method of converting coal to oil had been developed. The new process is 'extremely efficient and has no emissions' UTA scientist Brian Dennis stated. Mr. Dennis also stated that cost per barrel of oil was $28.84. Converting coal to oil needs to be extensively explored and could become crucial for America obtaining energy independence.

# NATURAL GAS

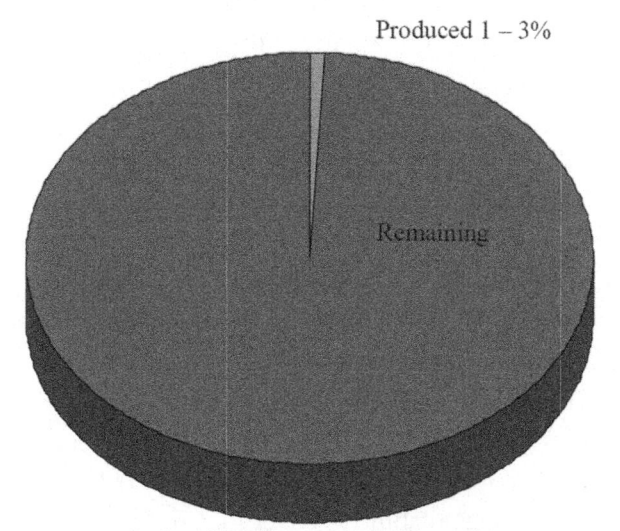

Produced 1 – 3%

Remaining

Courtesy of: U. S. Energy Information Agency, (EIA)

(Reference: 18.1)

According to the EIA, America has tremendous reserves of natural gas. As illustrated above, America has barely tapped America's natural gas resources. Much of the natural gas is tightly locked in shale and other materials that require fracking to release the natural gas. The down side of the tightly locked gas fields is the fact that each gas well could have a short production life. Due to this fact, as old wells become unproductive new gas wells will need to drilled in the same gas fields. The new wells will be necessary to maintain production and access the natural gas indicated in the pie chart. (As of 2013, industry experts state the new gas wells developed with horizontal drilling plus fracking are producing longer than expected.)

Natural gas has multiple uses plus having the least $CO_2$ emissions of all the fossil fuels. As of 2013, natural gas is used to generate approximately 25% of America's electricity. In many American homes natural gas is used for heating and cooking. Natural gas is also a raw material in fertilizers and a component in the manufacturing of plastics, pharmaceuticals, medical implants, electronic components, paints, sports equipment, cosmetics and the list continues.

Clearly, natural gas is extremely important to America's economy and energy needs. Due to the abundant supply of natural gas in America, there is little doubt that natural gas will become even more important. The U. S. Energy Information Agency, (EIA), estimates America will need an additional 250GW of new electric generating capacity between 2008 and 2035. Natural gas is projected to fuel the electric power plants responsible for up to 46% of the new electricity.

Natural gas can be, and in limited applications is being, used to fuel vehicles. Due to limited availability, vehicles currently fueled by natural gas operate within access of the vehicles' fueling facility. In 2013, many retail fuel dealers are either evaluating the opportunity to sell natural gas or are in the process of offering natural gas as a vehicle fuel. Time will tell as to the success of natural gas being widely used as a transportation fuel.

The major obstacles preventing natural gas from being widely used as a vehicle fuel are much like the old 'chicken or egg' situation. Since there are few vehicles setup to run on natural gas, there is little incentive for fuel retailers to sell natural gas. Then there is the fact that due to limited availability of natural gas outlets, there is little enticement for Americans to purchase vehicles that can run on natural gas.

Natural gas can be converted to liquids such as gasoline and diesel. Since the distribution channels for these fuels are established, the conversion of natural gas to liquids is a practical alternative for America to reduce its reliance on foreign oil.

# NUCLEAR POWER

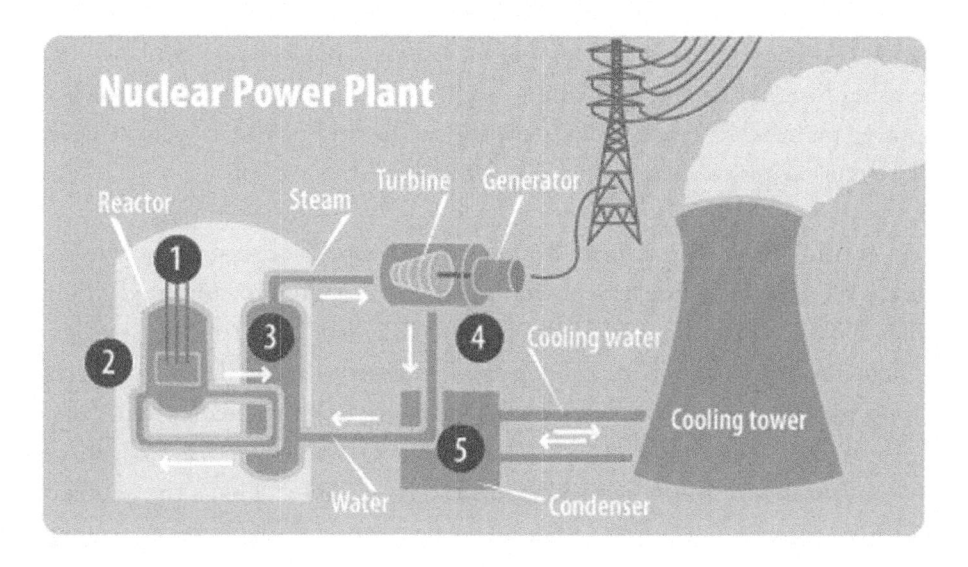

(Reference: 19.1)

When was the last time a nuclear power plant was built? The last nuclear power plant built was in 1996 and called the Watts Bar 1 located in Tennessee. In 2007, the Tennessee Valley Authority, (TVA), authorized the construction of a new nuclear power plant, (*Bellefonte nuclear power plant*), which is scheduled for completion in 2013. (There is a significant probability this new nuclear power plant will not be completed on time or maybe abandoned prior to completion.)

How many nuclear power plants in America? As of 2013, there are 65 commercially operating nuclear power plants with 104 nuclear reactors providing electricity for 31 states. In 2010 the largest nuclear power plant was the Palo Verde plant in Arizona with 3 reactors with a combined generating capacity of 3,942 Megawatts. In 2010, the smallest nuclear power plant was Fort Calhoun plant in Nebraska with a single reactor producing 478 Megawatts of electricity.

What is the average age of America's nuclear power plants? According to EIA, (U. S. Energy Information Agency), the average age of America's nuclear power plants is 32 years. How long is a nuclear power plant's operating license? Again, according to EIA, the initial license for a nuclear power plant is 40 years. What happens at the end of the 40 year license? The nuclear power plant can apply for a 20 year extension.

When did the U. S. Nuclear Regulatory Commission last authorize the construction of a nuclear power plant? According to an article published by CNN Money on February 9, 2012: *"The U.S. Nuclear Regulatory Commission approved licenses to build two new nuclear reactors Thursday, the first authorized in over 30 years."* The article also includes the statement; *"a coalition of nine mostly regional anti-nuclear groups say the current design is not safe. They plan on challenging Thursday's decision in federal court."* That's the problem with virtually any effort to make America energy independent. Anyone can file a court challenge which effectively shuts the project down until resolved. Thousands, if not millions of dollars are wasted responding to court challenges. It's time to trust the regulatory agencies to do their job and if they do not perform their duties responsibly, hold the regulatory agency accountable.

The two primary objections to nuclear power plants are: 1) No permanent location or method of disposing spent nuclear fuel rods. Currently the spent fuel is stored on location at the nuclear power plant. 2) Fear of nuclear power plant melt down. There have been significant advancements in technology to prevent melt downs. The nuclear power industry has one of the best safety records of all industries. But, as a result of the Three Mile Island event in 1979, no new construction permits were issued between 1979 and 2012. Until the Three Mile Island incident, the Nuclear Regulatory Board averaged 12 new construction permits per year.

The disposal of nuclear waste is without a doubt the most valid objection to nuclear power plants. There was a plan to store the spent nuclear fuel rods in Yucca Mountain located in Nevada. But the project was abandoned in 2009 due to controversy and legal challenges. Until there is a satisfactory disposal method or site, the nuclear power industry is unlikely to grow substantially.

# BIOFUELS

(Reference: 20.1)

The most basic need of mankind is food and water. Considering the fact that the world is over populated, how can any nation justify allocating vital farm land to be used in the production of crops for fuel? Biofuel production, (biofuel as used in this book includes ethanol), removes significant crop land from production of food. As of 2013, the primary product used in the U.S. to produce biofuels is corn. In addition to corn being a food consumed by humans, corn is also an important feedstock for poultry plus domestic animals used to produce beef and pork. Due to higher corn prices as a direct result of corn being used in the production of biofuels; the cost of food for Americans will continue to increase.

Biofuels are correctly classified as renewable. Classifying biofuels as a 'green fuel' is most likely incorrect. President Obama's EPA Administrator, Lisa Jackson, in reference to the use of biofuels, stated: "We can cut greenhouse gas emissions equivalent to taking 20 million cars off the road," during a conference call with reporters. What is the basis for this statement?

The following information is interesting upon closer examination: According to the U. S. Energy Information Agency, (EIA): "About 19.64 pounds of carbon dioxide ($CO_2$) are produced from burning a gallon of gasoline that does not contain ethanol." In the event the fuel is 90% gasoline and 10% ethanol, the EIA states: "_Under international agreement, $CO_2$ from ethanol and other biofuels are not counted at the tailpipe_, so burning a gallon of gasoline with 10% ethanol produces about 17.68 pounds of $CO_2$." The

## BIOFUELS

EIA also states: "About 22.38 pounds of $CO_2$ are produced by burning a gallon of diesel fuel." If the gallon of diesel contains 10% biodiesel, the EIA states: "Burning a gallon of "B10" (diesel fuel containing 10% biodiesel by volume) results in emission of about 20 pounds of $CO_2$."

The first question should be: "How much does a gallon of gasoline and diesel weigh?" The answer is 6.073 pounds for gasoline and a gallon of diesel weighs about 7.15 pounds. The next question is how can gasoline or diesel produce energy plus a byproduct, CO2 that is approximately 3 times the weight of the original fossil fuel? The commonsensical response is that it can't be done but upon closer examination the increased weight is logical. Carbon Dioxide is 1 part carbon which supplied by the fossil fuel, and 2 parts oxygen which is added to the fossil fuel during combustion. When you add the weight of the oxygen to the carbon, you arrive at a weight of approximately 3 times the fossil fuel being consumed. Since the oxygen originated from the atmosphere, the fossil fuel actually contributes to the atmosphere only the weight of the carbon burned. It seems that by stating a gallon of gasoline generates 19.64 pounds of CO2 makes the situation more ominous.

Now take a closer look at the EIA statement: ***"Under international agreement, $CO_2$ from ethanol and other biofuels are not counted at the tailpipe"***. Next note that the weight of CO2 emissions is reduced by precisely the same percentage as the amount of biofuels added to the fossil fuels, gasoline and diesel. The EIA statement indicates that there are CO2 emissions from biofuels but under international agreement these emissions are ignored. Also, not readily available in governmental data is the fact that fuel mileage is significantly less with biofuels when compared to the same quantity of fossil fuels. Remember that the next time you refuel your vehicle. (**Note:** ***The energy content of biodiesel is approximately 11% less than the same quantity of diesel. The energy content of ethanol is approximately 33% less than the same quantity of gasoline.***)

You have to be the judge. Is the government intentionally misleading Americans as to the actual atmospheric damage being done by burning fossil fuels? Is the government over stating the reduction in atmospheric $CO_2$ emissions as a result of adding biofuels to fossil fuels? Is there a government conspiracy to promote an environmental agenda or other self-serving scheme? These questions do not question the validity of a correlation between atmospheric $CO_2$ and the change in earth's average temperature. It's just time for elected and appointed government officials to stop misleading Americans with half truths and outright deceit. Think about it: Either America's elected leaders are performing as ventriloquist's dummies and 'mouthing' what their controlling 'ventriloquist' utter without thought as to whether the statement is correct; or America's elected leaders are intentionally lying to Americans. The question must be asked: Are these the people that should be leading America?

Clearly, biofuels do emit $CO_2$ when combustion occurs. Add to this the $CO_2$ that is emitted when the product, corn in the case of ethanol and soybeans in the case of biodiesel, are planted, cultivated, irrigated, harvested, transported to the processing plant, processed and finally transferred to the fuel distribution terminal. Now add to this the lost capacity of the land being used to cultivate the biofuel material no longer containing the plant life that was performing as a $CO_2$ sink, (absorb atmospheric $CO_2$). If the land was originally used for food crops, other lands will need to be planted to replace the food crop the biofuel crop eliminated. This means, either in America or another country, another parcel of land has been cultivated for food production purposes. There is no way biofuels reduce atmospheric $CO_2$ emissions. When every aspect of the production of biofuels is considered, it is highly probable biofuels substantially increase $CO_2$ emissions when compared to same energy output as fossil fuels produce.

If biofuels were produced from agriculture byproducts, such as corn stalks, wheat stems, cotton plants remaining after the cotton has been harvested, biofuels could contribute to America's energy independence.

## BIOFUELS

Additionally, if biofuels are produced from food waste, such as cooking oils, there could be significant benefits for the planet. That said, the net biofuel CO2 emissions verses the CO2 emissions of fossil fuels would still be open to debate.

One additional concern is the potential of engine damage caused by ethanol. Ethanol readily absorbs moisture. Additional as outside temperatures decrease, ethanol can separate from gasoline and form 'globs' of a jell like mass which will settle in the bottom of a fuel tank and then clog and damage engines and fuel systems. Then there is the fact that ethanol is a conductor of electricity which can result in significant corrosion of fuel systems, especially in fuel blends greater than 10 percent ethanol.

Finally, America has more than enough naturally occurring fossil fuel resources to power America for centuries without biofuels. All Americans need to do is insist America's elected leaders develop these abundant resources in a manner that is in the best interest of most Americans and to do so as quickly as possible.

**NOTE:** This section on biofuels has been extremely difficult to write. As a young man, I worked on farms and ranches. One of my best friends is a farmer. I've owned a farm, which in no way makes me a farmer, (I did not have to survive on what my farm produced.) I've designed and developed computer systems for agricultural businesses. Family farmers work hard to produce products that are subject to free market supply and demand pricing. It is difficult for a family to produce the income required to maintain and retain family farms plus provide the necessities of life. Throw in unpredictable Mother Nature and the family farm picture becomes even bleaker. Personally, I believe the family farmer deserves all possible markets for the products produced on the farm. But as previously stated, this book is being written from the position of what is best for most Americans.

# HYDRO-POWER

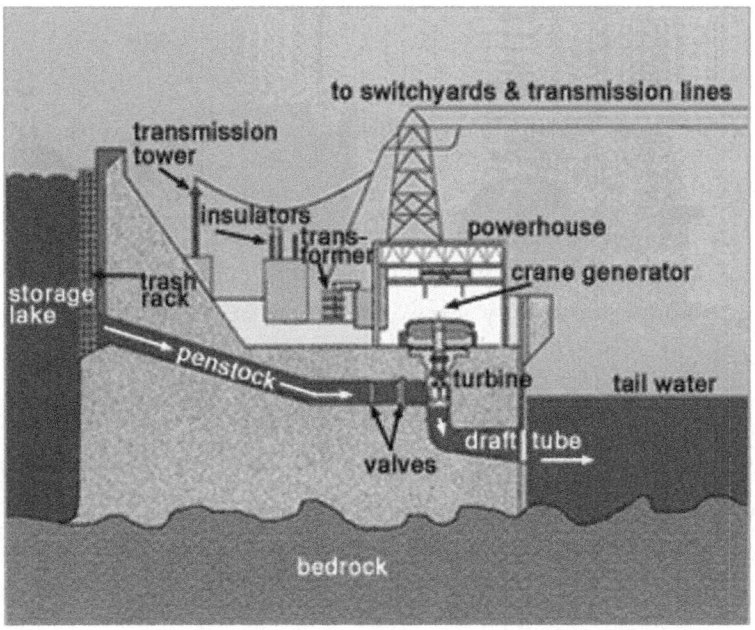

**Above:** Hydroelectric power generation process

(Reference: 21.1)

Water is currently the leading renewable energy source in the production of electricity. Hydro-electric power plants produce very little CO2 and are a cheap source for the generation of electricity. The down side is the fact that by damming rivers and streams there can be a significant negative impact on fish, other wildlife plus other environmental transformations.

According to the U. S. Energy Information Agency, (EIA): "Nearly all of the hydroelectric capacity was built before the mid-1970s, and much of it is at dams operated by federal government agencies." The EIA also states: "Hydroelectric generation increases in some years and decreases in others, primarily due to variation in the amounts of rainfall and melting snowfall occurring in watersheds where major hydroelectric dams are located." Power generation of existing hydro-electricity power plants may be increased over time through advances in hydro-electric technology.

Considering all the renewable energy options, hydro power is the only one that can compete successfully with fossil fuels and nuclear energy. The limitation of hydro power generated electricity is that it can only be produced where there is an adequate source of water. This limitation can result in the building of long, expensive power lines that also substantially decrease the power delivered to consumers. The decrease in power generated at the hydro facility and delivered to the consumer is due to the resistance in the power lines.

Since there are limited new opportunities for hydro power, the electricity produced by water will likely continue to decrease as a percentage of the total electricity produced in America's future.

# GEO-THERMAL POWER

(Reference: 22.1)

What is geothermal energy? According to the U. S. Energy Information Agency, (EIA): "The word geothermal comes from the Greek words *geo* (earth) and *therme* (heat). So, geothermal energy is heat from within the Earth. We can recover this heat as steam or hot water and use it to heat buildings or generate electricity." "Naturally occurring large areas of hydrothermal resources are called **geothermal reservoirs**. Most geothermal reservoirs are deep underground with no visible clues showing above ground. But geothermal energy sometimes finds its way to the surface in the form of:

- **Volcanoes** and **fumaroles** (holes where volcanic gases are released)
- **Hot springs**
- **Geysers**"

# GEO-THERMAL POWER

Where are geothermal reservoirs useable as power sources located? According to the EIA: "The most active geothermal resources are usually found along major plate boundaries where earthquakes and volcanoes are concentrated. Most of the geothermal activity in the world occurs in an area called the **Ring of Fire**. This area encircles the Pacific Ocean." The west coast of America is located on the eastern edge of the Ring of Fire.

Due to the location and population the EIA states: *"Most of the geothermal power plants in the United States are located in the western states and Hawaii, where geothermal energy resources are close to the surface. California generates the most electricity from geothermal energy."* The EIA adds: *"The United States leads the world in electricity generation with geothermal power. In 2012, U.S. geothermal power plants produced about 17 billion kilowatt-hours (kWh), or 0.4% of total U.S. electricity generation."* Due to the limited location of geothermal reservoirs, the use of geothermal power will continue to be primarily a western U. S. energy resource.

# SOLAR

(Reference: 23.1)

According to the U. S. Energy Information Agency, (EIA): "Unlike other renewable sources, a significant amount of solar power is generated by small-scale, customer-sited installations like rooftop solar (or, distributed generation). According to the *Annual Energy Outlook 2013*, these small solar facilities are projected to generate an estimated 14.13 billion kilowatt hours of electricity in 2013. The availability of solar energy has daily and seasonal patterns, so resulting generation fluctuates widely."

Due to the limitation of solar power to the times which there is adequate sunlight, solar power is not likely to be more than a supplemental source of electricity. Solar power can reduce America's fossil fuel requirements. The question is at what cost to electrical consumers? Is the cost of the solar power system offset by the decrease in the cost of fossil fuels? The answers to these questions are likely the reason that most solar generated electricity is by consumers. The government has passed regulations requiring electricity producing companies to 'buy back' electricity produced by customers using renewable energy technology. Solar power is a way for electricity customers to reduce power costs by 'selling' back their solar generated electricity to the electric power company.

# WIND

(Reference: 24.1)

According to the U. S. Energy Information Agency, (EIA): "*The amount of installed wind generation dramatically increased in the past decade, due in part to Federal financial incentives and State government mandates, especially renewable portfolio standards. The availability of wind energy has daily and seasonal patterns, so resulting generation fluctuates widely.*"

As stated by the EIA, electricity generated by wind is inconsistent. If there is insufficient wind, no electricity will be generated. As with solar, wind generated electricity is a supplemental energy source which reduces the fuel requirements of more traditional electricity generation methods. As with solar, is there a cost saving or are the additional costs of wind generators passed on to tax payers and electricity consumers? Unlike solar, wind generators are not likely to be implemented by the electricity customers.

# BIOMASS

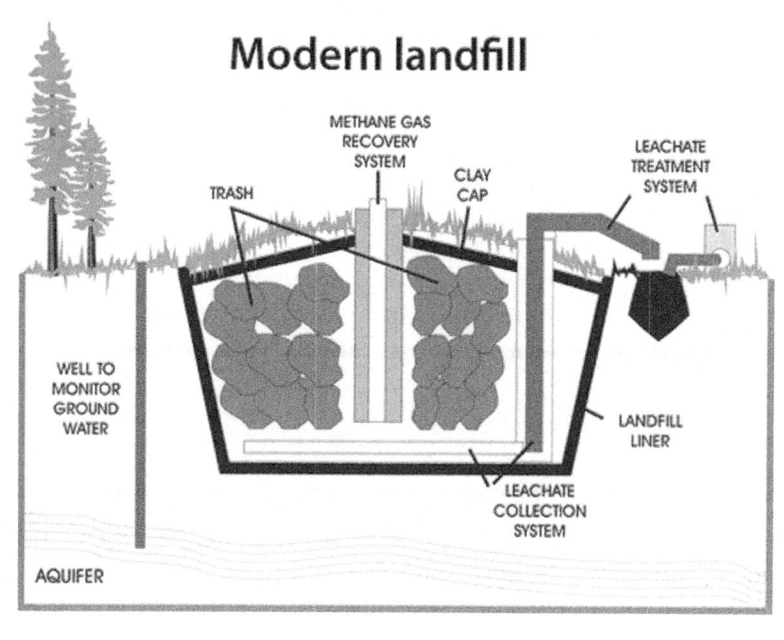

## Modern landfill

(Reference: 25.1)

According to the U. S. Energy Information Agency, (EIA): "Biomass waste is mostly municipal solid waste which is burned as fuel to run power plants." The EIA continues: "Most of the electricity from wood biomass is generated at lumber and paper mills. These mills use their own wood waste to provide much of their own steam and electricity needs."

Biomass appears to have minimal relevance for America's future energy needs.

# RENEWABLE ENERGY GOVERNMENT INCENTIVES

According to the U. S. EIA in 2012, 12% of the U. S. Electricity was Produced with Renewable Energy.

| | |
|---|---|
| Solar | 1% |
| Geothermal | 3% |
| Biomass Waste | 4% |
| Biomass Wood | 8% |
| Wind | 28% |
| Hydropower | 56% |

(Reference: 26.1)

According to the U. S. Energy Information Agency, (EIA): *"China leads the world in total electricity generation from renewable energy due to its recent massive additions to hydroelectric capacity, followed closely by the United States, Brazil, and Canada. However, the United States produces the most electricity from non-hydroelectric renewable sources, followed by China and Germany."*

Why doesn't the U. S. use more renewable energy in the production of electricity? According to the EIA: "**Renewable Energy Technologies Are Often Expensive:** *Renewable energy power plants can be more expensive to build and to operate (in terms of dollars per unit of electricity output) than natural gas or even coal plants."* The EIA continues: "**Renewable Resources Are Often Geographically Remote:** *Many renewable resources are available only in remote areas, and building transmission lines to deliver power to large metropolitan areas is expensive."*

In spite of the cost and location issues with renewable energy, according to the EIA, the Federal government along with several State governments have enacted the following three kinds of policies to increase the use of renewable fuels: "(1) **Tax credits:** The Renewable Electricity Production Tax Credit, a federal incentive, has encouraged a major increase in generation from wind and other eligible renewable sources. (2) **Targets:** Many states have Renewable Portfolio Standards (RPS), which require electricity providers to generate or acquire a certain portion of their power supplies from renewable sources. However, many RPS programs have "escape clauses" if renewable generation exceeds a cost threshold. (3) **Markets:** A number of states have built Renewable Energy Certificates/Credits (RECs) into their Renewable Portfolio Standards. This allows electricity providers to sell renewable energy certificates/credits. Some states have made REC markets mandatory, requiring electricity providers to produce or acquire renewable generation to reduce reliance on fossil fuels to generate electricity."

### Electricity Generation by Renewable Energy Tax Credit Table

| Resource Type | Begin Construction Deadline | Credit Amount |
|---|---|---|
| Wind | December 31, 2013 | 2.3¢/kWh |
| Closed-Loop Biomass | December 31, 2013 | 2.3¢/kWh |
| Open-Loop Biomass | December 31, 2013 | 1.1¢/kWh |
| Geothermal Energy | December 31, 2013 | 2.3¢/kWh |
| Landfill Gas | December 31, 2013 | 1.1¢/kWh |
| Municipal Solid Waste | December 31, 2013 | 1.1¢/kWh |
| Qualified Hydroelectric | December 31, 2013 | 1.1¢/kWh |
| Marine and Hydrokinetic (150 kW or larger)** | December 31, 2013 | 1.1¢/kWh |

The duration of the credit is generally 10 years after the date the facility is placed in service, but there are two exceptions:

* Open-loop biomass, geothermal, small irrigation hydro, landfill gas and municipal solid waste combustion facilities placed into service after October 22, 2004, and before enactment of the "Energy Policy Act of 2005", on August 8, 2005, are only eligible for the credit for a five-year period.
* Open-loop biomass facilities placed in service before October 22, 2004, are eligible for a five-year period beginning January 1, 2005.

**Courtesy: Energy.gov**

(Reference 26.2)

**In addition to the electricity production tax credits shown in the table the government may provide construction or purchase tax credits of 30%.**

Tax credits used properly can create jobs and advance technology. Shouldn't the tax credits be limited to projects using supplies and materials 100% American made? What is going to happen with the renewable energy projects when the incentives end? Is it possible for corporate executives to develop business models that create profits based on the governmental incentives? Would the businesses created due to the governmental incentives be able to continue producing electricity without the inducements? Prior to allowing a renewable energy power system to receive tax credits, wouldn't it be beneficial for the project to demonstrate the ability to remain in operation once the tax credits expire?

# CONCLUSION

Americans must confront the fact that America's elected leaders, as well as many World leaders; have only a 'Plan A'. That plan is to reduce consumption of fossil fuels in an effort to reduce atmospheric CO2 emissions. The fact the atmosphere presently contains more than enough CO2 to dramatically alter Earth's climate is being ignored or avoided. America's leaders appear to be side stepping the actions America must put in place to adapt to the inescapable climate change currently underway. How is America going to create an economy that will sustain America while adapting to climate change? Unless Americans accept the fact that 'Plan A' is no more than an exercise in futility and aggressively pursue a 'Plan B', America's days are numbered. The Fuel America Now, (FAN), energy plan is the foundation on which a 'Plan B' can be created.

The following is not intended as an attack on President Obama. There are plenty of examples of his predecessors also mismanaging America's natural resources. It's just that President Obama is in office at the time this book is being written.

**President Obama, March 30, 2011:** *"We cannot keep going from shock to trance on the issue of energy security, rushing to propose action when gas prices rise, then hitting the snooze button when they fall again. The United States of America cannot afford to bet our long-term prosperity and security on a resource that will eventually run out. Not anymore. Not when the cost to our economy, our country, and our planet is so high. Not when your generation needs us to get this right. It is time to do what we can to secure our energy future."*

**President Obama, March 15, 2012** *"We can't have an energy strategy for the last century that traps us in the past. We need an energy strategy for the future – an all-of-the-above strategy for the 21st century that develops every source of American-made energy."*

In 2011, President Obama makes it clear that he believes fossil fuels are detrimental to America's future. Then approximately 1 year later he states that America needs '*an energy strategy for the future – an all-of-the-above-strategy for the 21st century that develops every source of American-made energy*." This is a clear case of saying what the voter wants to hear. Once elected, the politician, in this case President Obama, can continue doing what they originally intended. As most Americans know: **President Obama is doing everything he can to promote green and/or renewable energy plus encourage regulatory obstructions whenever and wherever possible that will hinder the development of America's fossil fuels.** Is President Obama managing America's natural resources in a way that is in the best interest of most Americans? Only if you want to make sure the American life style becomes just a memory.

As you can see from President Obama's statements, the government uses two basic arguments to justify investing tax payer monies in 'green' and/or 'renewable' energy:

1. *Carbon Dioxide, (CO2), emitted by fossil fuels is the primary cause of global warming.*
2. *There is a finite amount of fossil fuels; with crude oil reserves being rapidly diminished resulting in escalating oil prices.*

The first argument is correct and verifiable from data collected from samples of ice existing for hundreds of thousands of years validating the historical correlation between atmospheric CO2 and global temperature change. **The glaring problem, which is not getting the essential public attention, is the fact there is presently more than enough CO2 in the atmosphere to make global temperatures extremely inhospitable for humans.** Reducing CO2 emissions by decreasing the use of fossil fuels will <u>at best</u> only delay the inevitable global warming. Also, due to human over population, the emission of CO2, (emitters), into the atmosphere will

# CONCLUSION

continue to exceed the CO2 absorbed by the earth, (sinks). An undeniable fact: The current atmospheric CO2 levels, if not reduced, will likely end human life as we know it.

The second premise used to justify the government's position on developing 'green' and/or 'renewable' energy resources is that Earth contains a finite amount of fossil fuels which will be exhausted in a relatively short period. Question: Since oil is a hydrocarbon and hydrogen and carbon are elements which are not destroyed when oil based energy products are consumed; how can the world run out of oil or other fossil fuels? No question, the world will eventually run out of naturally occurring crude oil resources. Since the chemical composition of oil is so simple, what keeps mankind from reassembling the hydrogen and carbon elements, creating synthetic oil? The premise the world will run out of fossil fuels is intentionally misleading.

Oil is the fossil fuel which has the greatest impact on human life and appears to be the fossil fuel that will be exhausted first. As previously stated, there is no substitute for oil, not now and not in the foreseeable future. Since oil cannot be replaced, wouldn't it make more sense for America to develop technology that will provide oil from sources other than the traditional oil well drilling and pumping?

America has more than enough fossil fuel resources to provide America oil for literally hundreds of years at costs significantly less than often quoted on World energy markets. As America consumes its natural fossil fuel resources, America has more than enough time to create the technology required to produce synthetic oil in commercial quantities. Additionally, since the continuation of human life depends on technology to monitor and control atmospheric CO2, it is highly probable some of the reclaimed atmospheric CO2 can be converted to oil as needed making oil a renewable energy resource.

It is well past time for America to develop all its energy resources. These energy resources must be used to create a strong, sustainable economy that will provide the financial resources essential for the development of the technology to monitor and control atmospheric $CO_2$. At current atmospheric $CO_2$ levels, global warming will continue and unless existing atmospheric $CO_2$ levels are reduced, the future of humans has already been set. America needs to develop the technology required to monitor and control atmospheric $CO_2$. Concurrently, or as soon as possible, America must also develop the technology to convert atmospheric $CO_2$ to synthetic oil. This technology will need to be licensed to other countries. Try to imagine how quickly the atmospheric $CO_2$ could be reduced if other countries participated in atmospheric $CO_2$ monitoring and control. What better incentive to get involved in controlling atmospheric $CO_2$ than the ability to produce oil from the atmosphere eliminating the importation of overpriced crude oil from oil producing countries? Obviously, the process to convert atmospheric $CO_2$ to oil will be aggressively opposed by oil producing countries, major oil companies and environmentalists.

At this point you should realize that our elected leaders have grossly mismanaged America's energy resources plus the economy and environment. Unfortunately, their mismanagement has had little impact on their lives as well as the lives of Americans involved in the Washington D. C. governmental complex. If you have any doubts, take a look at how the Washington D. C. area weathered the 'Great Recession' which according to the National Bureau of Economic Research began in 2007. As of 2013 many Americans outside Washington D.C. still endure lingering hardships of the great or long recession. What are Americans to do?

First accept the fact that elected members of Congress, as well as the President, are impervious to America's economic down turns. Add to this list of people immune to America's adverse economic situation, rich Americans, many with significant political influence. (In no way is this meant to debase being rich. It is just making it clear that the fluctuations

## CONCLUSION

in the economy has less impact on more financially secure Americans.) America is built on a capitalistic system that encourages hard working Americans to improve their lives to a level not possible in any other country. The problem is that politically moderate, hard working Americans have voluntarily relinquished their futures to extremists on both ends of the political spectrum. This is a situation that must not continue.

Rather than vote along party lines, (Democrat or Republican), or blindly support liberal or conservative ideals, Americans must declare their independence and support ideas and proposals that are in the best interest of most Americans. Americans can no longer fall victim to politically strategic word play, (words that sound good but little meaning), and then standby while government continues to operate as it has for decades. It's time to provide elected leaders with clear instructions as to what is best for most Americans and if the elected leaders ignore the instructions, vote them out of office.

The following are two realistic scenarios based on the action or inaction of voting Americans. No one can accurately forecast the future. That said, everyone should realize that there will be an outcome relative to an action or inaction. The following are two prospective outcomes. The first is what could occur if America does not change course. The second is an achievable outcome if America revises its present course.

If Americans do not make radical changes to how they vote, America will continue with 'Plan A', ignoring the impact of existing $CO_2$ levels. As a result of America not changing its current course the following scenario could occur: America's government will continue to spend more than it takes in, allowing government debt to increase at an accelerating rate. As the debt continues to increase, America's way of life will deteriorate at a rapidly increasing rate. Fuel costs will increase to the point that many Americans will no longer be able to afford personal vehicles. Vehicle manufacturing will falter, resulting in a domino effect which will dramatically increase unemployment. More and more American jobs will continue to disappear. Farmers will reduce farming lands due to unaffordable fuel and chemical costs. Increasing numbers of Americans will be looking to the government for assistance in meeting life's necessities, (food, clothing and shelter). Inevitably, America's debt load will reach the point that it cannot be repaid, ending America's Democracy and capitalistic economy. America's downfall will result in worldwide famine due to the loss of America's production and export of grain and other food products. As a result of the loss of America's agriculture exports, famine will engulf the world resulting in the fall of many governments followed by complete anarchy. Finally, global warming will continue, eventually creating an environment completely inhospitable for human life.

If Americans do make the necessary changes to how they vote, America will do whatever is necessary to provide the energy to fuel a strong American economy. America will gain a competitive economic advantage over other countries due to America's unparalleled energy resources. Industry will return to America creating jobs for all Americans. Most Americans will be able to live the American dream. Americans on government subsidies will be able to become employed and turn into taxpaying Americans. Increased tax revenue along with significant energy royalty income plus revenue resulting from an improved balance in trade will allow America to balance the budget and pay down national debt. America will have the financial means essential to aggressively attack global warming by developing the technology required to monitor and control the atmospheric $CO_2$ levels. The new technology will artificially balance the carbon exchange between earth and the atmosphere. By maintaining atmospheric $CO_2$ at desired levels, global temperatures can be sustained at levels which are in the best interest for human life. Other countries will benefit from the American technological advances and create better lives for their citizens.

## CONCLUSION

As previously stated no one can accurately forecast the future. You may envision different scenarios but hopefully, you realize that America cannot continue without a realistic, long term energy policy. Without exception, America's energy policy must be in the best interest of most Americans. The following section of this book is an effort to create the basics of an energy plan that will not only benefit most Americans, but also provide an opportunity to defeat global warming.

# FUEL AMERICA NOW! – ENERGY PLAN

The Fuel America Now, (FAN), energy plan is intended to develop America's natural resources in a manner which is in the best interest of most Americans. FAN is designed to create the foundation for the creation of America's energy policy. The FAN energy plan will assist America in the development of an expanding, robust economy essential to provide a competitive edge in attracting industry and jobs back to America. Once a realistic energy plan has been implemented, it should limit the extent to which presently elected as well as future elected leaders can mismanage America's energy resources.

1. **Global warming.** The FAN energy plan is founded on the fact there is already more than enough $CO_2$ in the atmosphere to end, or virtually end human life at some point in the future. Also, regardless of America's use, reduced use or non use of fossil fuels, the emission of $CO_2$ into the atmosphere by humans and other natural causes significantly exceeds the ability of earth's sinks, (trees, plants, ocean), to remove and sequester atmospheric $CO_2$. FAN concedes the reality that life on earth is carbon based due to the fact carbon is responsible for all earth's life forms. Carbon gives life and carbon, (in the form of atmospheric $CO_2$), can also end life on earth. Unless humans develop the technology required to monitor and control atmospheric $CO_2$, mankind's continued existence is doubtful at best.

2. **Prepare for climate change.** During the time required to develop and implement the technology required to monitor and control atmospheric $CO_2$, America will need to make the adjustments required to adapt to changes in climate. Farming will have to deal with major changes. Regions that previously received regular rain fall will experience droughts. Areas that were dry may receive extra moisture. Regions that are already hot in summer may become

excessively hot. Coastal cities will experience higher tides than normal. Many other adjustments to life will have to be made due to current and future climate changes. America must be prepared financially and technologically to adapt to climate change.

3. **Over population.** The root cause of excessive atmospheric $CO_2$ emissions is first and foremost the result of human over population. If human population continues to grow, at some point the earth's ability to support mankind will be exceeded. America is fortunate in the fact that its population does not surpass America's natural resources required to support the current population. The problem is America's population continues to grow, primarily as result of immigration, plus the fact the new immigrants tend to have larger families. America's energy policy should include regulations designed to manage immigration plus encourage smaller families. An example would be to limit personal tax deductions to 4 per family, 2 adults and 2 children. If a couple wants a larger family, that's their business but they will only receive tax deductions for 2 children. Also, apply the similar limitations to individuals on public assistance.

4. **If America is to fill highly skilled positions with Americans, America will have to make significant changes in advanced education and training.** Automation has significantly reduced the need for unskilled and minimally skilled employees. As America's economy improves, there will be a serious need for highly educated and trained employees. At least initially, many of these positions may require the immigration of the required talent. America will need to rethink its trade school and college education system. How can a society justify offering fully paid college scholarships, including room and board plus a spending allowance, to students based solely on their abilities throwing, catching, hitting or running with a ball; while requiring highly motivated,

capable American students to incur significant debt to obtain a trade school or college education?

5. **Reduce greenhouse gas emissions.** The FAN energy plan underscores the need to develop technology to reduce CO2 and other greenhouse gas emissions as a result of consuming fossil fuels. At the same time, Americans must realize that regardless of how much America reduces its green house emissions, **global** green house emissions will continue to increase. According to NOAA, the year 2012 has clearly revealed, even as America reduced its CO2 emissions, global CO2 emissions not only continued to increase; global CO2 emissions increased at a near record rate.

6. **Remove America's oil, coal and natural gas from the influence of world energy markets.** America's energy resources need to be limited to use in the United States. Only American individuals, companies and organizations with the facilities to take delivery of the product; then consume, process and/or market the fossil fuel products within the boarders and territories of America, can purchase America's fossil fuels. Energy speculation by financial investors using U.S. markets or operating within America's boarders is illegal. America's fossil fuel resources must be developed and consumed in a manner that is in the best interest of most Americans, both living now and not yet born. America must use its fossil fuel resources to provide a competitive edge in the international market. By doing so, America's low energy costs will create an economic environment that will return industry and jobs that were previously lost to countries with lower wages.

If America allows its oil prices to be influenced by world markets, even after achieving energy independence, energy prices would never become stable and manageable by most Americans. If America's energy prices are allowed to fluctuate based on world events, America's wealth would simply be transferred from average Americans to oil producers and marketers. America's energy independence would be meaningless to most Americans.

The Federal Energy Regulatory Commission, (FERC), oversees specific aspects of electric power generation, hydropower facilities; natural gas pipelines, transportation and storage, plus oil transportation. The FERC regulates electric power generation and distribution more closely than the other energy products. Since fossil fuels will not be subject to open market pricing, the prices will need to be set by FERC or other regulatory agency. Energy is a necessity for modern life and needs to be regulated to prevent the price gouging Americans are currently experiencing. Energy producers, refiners, carriers, marketers and retailers must be able to make a profit. The regulation of fossil fuels could follow the electricity model that has served America and industry well for decades.

7. **America's crude oil exports are generally prohibited by statute: "The Energy Policy and Conservation Act of 1975" (P.L. 94-163, EPCA) directs the President to restrict the export of crude oil.** There are loop holes and exceptions to this statute that need to be closed. Also, the statute needs to be broadened to include all fossil fuels. In addition to preserving America's natural resources for Americans, by becoming energy independent plus eliminating the export of America's fossil fuels, America will become immune to world events that now result in major fluctuations in energy costs for all Americans.

8. **Limit exports of refined energy products.** Refined oil products can only be exported if demand for the product in America has been met plus the production of the product to be exported is due to an imbalance in demand for other products produced in the

production cycle. If America's need for a specific energy product, i.e. gasoline, is at a level that requires the production of other energy products; i.e. diesel, heating oil, propane, at levels that exceed America's market requirements, the excess production can be exported. In the event coal, natural gas or other fossil fuel is converted to oil, the oil produced will be subject to the same restrictions as oil produced from conventional oil wells and methods.

9. **Limit import of crude oil for refining.** Crude oil can only be imported if: (1) America's need for energy exceeds the production of America's natural resources. (2) If America's need for energy and oil related products has been fully supplied and refinery processing capacity exceeds the production capacity required to meet America's needs. In which case, the products produced from the imported oil or other fossil fuel resource, can be exported without restrictions.

10. **Set a minimum price for oil and other fossil fuels.** Since America imports approximately 25% of foreign oil production, as America reduces its imports, there is a probability that the world price of oil will drop, maybe drop dramatically or even 'crash'.

    When imported oil prices increased significantly in the 1970s, American oil companies increased efforts to develop America's oil shale. Then in the early 1980s, oil prices dropped considerably, making oil produced from oil shale unprofitable. On May 2, 1982, Exxon cancelled its participation in the development of America's oil shale. The date is referred to as 'Black Sunday' by locals in western Colorado since more than 2,000 workers lost their jobs on that date. America cannot allow the situation to be repeated. There has to be a minimum price for a barrel of oil that will allow America's non-conventional oil resources to be developed profitably. The minimum price for a barrel of oil could be $60 or less. In the event the world market price for oil drops below the minimum price, there would be a tariff on imports equal to the difference in price.

There is a problem with tariffs. The United States is a member of the World Trade Organization, (WTO), which provides a forum for nations to file complaints against other nations 'unfairly' using tariffs to suppress trade. There is little doubt a complaint would be filed in the event America applied a tariff on imported oil. America could use the anti-dumping defense in this situation. America's position would be that oil prices were decreased to prevent America from developing its energy resources.

11. **Eliminate government regulations that hinder development of America's fossil fuel resources.** The FAN energy plan stresses the fact that environmental regulations must be enacted or current environmental regulations changed to encourage development of America's energy resources in a manner that minimizes the harmful environmental impact. Public lands under the management of the Bureau of Land Management, (BLM), must be opened for the exploration and development of America's oil shale as well as other fossil fuels.

It is impossible to develop most fossil fuel resources without negatively impacting the environment. The negative impact on the environment resulting from developing fossil fuel resources must be minimized utilizing existing technology. Unless the environmental damage resulting from developing fossil fuel resources have a proven and substantial harmful impact on humans, the development of the fossil fuel resource cannot be blocked.

12. **Limit the time a holder of a government energy lease is allowed to develop the lease.** America cannot allow large energy companies to stock pile energy leases. Once a lease is issued the

lease owner must begin development within a specified period of time. The lease holder will be required to be in production by a designated date. Plus, if there is sufficient data available to support the anticipated production volume, the lease owner will be required to be in production at an expected volume or be able to justify the failure to produce at the projected volume. Leases to develop energy resources on Federal lands must be made available as necessary to sustain America's economic requirements.

13. **Legal challenges to the development of America's fossil fuel resources limited to Federal Courts.** The FAN energy plan prevents the filing of trivial suits designed to interfere with the development of America's fossil fuels in local courts which could issue baseless injunctions. If there is legal justification for challenging, halting or revising the development of specific energy resources, the case must be presented before and ruled on by a federal court. The loser of the court challenge will be liable for all court costs plus damages to the opposing party.

14. **Promote research and development.** The FAN energy plan emphasizes the fact that America's government should provide financial incentives for the research and development of technology that monitors and controls atmospheric $CO_2$. Additionally, America's government should offer incentives for the development of technology that reduces $CO_2$ emissions as a result of the consumption of fossil fuels. The development of businesses specializing in the development of new energy technology should mostly be left to private enterprise. The project to monitor and control atmospheric $CO_2$ will likely have to be a government project due to the massive cost of research, development and implementation with little or no possibility of generating profits.

Once the technology required to monitor and control atmospheric $CO_2$ has been developed, the next logical step would be to convert a portion of the captured $CO_2$ into synthetic oil. This will allow carbon to be recycled and significantly reduce the need for conventional and non-conventional fossil fuels. Until the atmospheric $CO_2$ has been reduced to a level that will eliminate the threat of global warming, a significant portion of the captured atmospheric $CO_2$ will have to the sequestered, (stored in the earth).

15. **America cannot continue to jeopardize the future of Americans on technology that does not exist and may never exist.** For years there has been the rumor of a battery that could allow vehicles to travel hundreds of miles without recharging was on the threshold of being developed. If solar and wind energy arrays are to be stand alone rather than be supplemental electricity producers, there will need to be major advances in electrical storage devices, (i.e. batteries). If America continues to ignore its available energy resources while waiting on advances in technology, there is a high probability American's will continue to struggle in a weak and unstable economy. Plus, climate change will continue unabated.

16. **America will need to responsibly manage the significant influx of cash that will be the result of a strong economy.** The world's oil producing countries, by and large, have squandered the considerable wealth their oil production and sales have created. America cannot repeat the mistake. The FAN energy plan is structured to manage America's energy resources in a manner that is in the best interest of most Americans. With 'cheap and plentiful' energy, America will attract manufacturing that will create goods and services that will be marketed internationally, generating a trade surplus. Americans share the 'space ship' we call earth with

other humans. Americans will need to use a significant portion of the wealth generated from America's robust economy to create the technology required to monitor and control atmospheric CO2; eliminating the global warming threat. The bottom line is that the world can benefit from America's success as a result of Americans developing America's natural energy resources.

17. **When America's economy enters into a recessionary or inflationary period, if the government regulates fossil fuel prices, the cost of fuel could be decreased or increased as required to alter the economy.** This is an idea which will create a lot of controversy but really deserves considerable thought and consideration. American consumers are particularly sensitive to changes in energy costs, especially when it comes time to refuel their vehicles. There could be an argument for regulating energy costs rather than printing money or controlling interest rates. Furthermore, since energy prices influence virtually every product and service required for modern life; a minimal change in energy cost could significantly impact America's economy. With the dollar stabilized, people on fixed income would be able to live their lives rather than live in fear about the loss of purchasing power of their incomes.

**The FAN energy plan is a straightforward document when compared to the energy plans put forth by President Obama and his predecessor President Bush.** The FAN energy plan puts forth thoughtful steps that can lead America into a future that will benefit not only hard working, self-reliant Americans but also all mankind. Anyone reading FAN could be offended or opposed to at least one of the FAN energy plan segments. Anyone opposing a FAN energy plan component needs to offer an alternative proposal rather than unfounded opposition. **Think about it, if the FAN energy plan did not invoke controversy, it would be just another meaningless, politically correct energy policy that will do nothing for anyone.** When it comes to energy, based on past experience; the political approach may be different, but the unproductive end result will be the same, regardless of the political party in control.

President Bush's plan, as presented in the next section, was signed into law on August 8, 2005. What has it done for America's energy needs and economy? Was President Bush's energy plan a significant contributor to the Great Recession which was in full force at the end of President Bush's second term?

Now President Obama has put forth his *'Blueprint for a Secure Energy Future'*, (shown immediately after President Bush's energy plan). Is the Blueprint a lot of political jargon with little substance? Decide for yourself. President Obama's first section states: "Expand Safe and Responsible Domestic Oil and Gas Development and Production". Considering President Obama's position on fossil fuels, do you think he will actually authorize any significant development? If it were not for the advent of horizontal drilling and fracking, Americans would be far worse off than they are now. President Obama tries to take credit for the increased oil production but most Americans realize the increase in oil and natural gas production occurred in spite of him. This is not intended as an attack on President Obama, it's just a fact.

The bottom line is neither President Bush nor President Obama submitted energy plans that would benefit the self reliant, hard working Americans. The Fuel America Now energy plan, (FAN), is based on the fact that fossil fuels are required in the foreseeable future and will be America's primary source of energy for the predictable future. $CO_2$ emissions will continue to exceed $CO_2$ captured by sinks and sequestered until humans develop the required technology to monitor and control atmospheric $CO_2$. The FAN energy plan also emphasizes the fact that if $CO_2$ is the primary cause of climate change, there is already more than enough $CO_2$ in the atmosphere to make the world too warm for most humans. Rather than focus solely on reducing future $CO_2$ emissions as the solution for global warming, ('Plan A'), FAN focuses on correcting the atmospheric damage that already exists and then manage the atmospheric CO2 at a level which humans seem to thrive, ('Plan B').

**"If humanity wishes to preserve a planet similar to that on which civilization developed and to which life on Earth is adapted, paleoclimate evidence and ongoing climate change suggest that CO2 will need to be reduced from its current 385 ppm to at most 350 ppm."** (CO2 exceeded 400 ppm in 2013.) (Quoted from: 'Target Atmospheric CO2: Where Should Humanity Aim? By: James Hansen,1,2* Makiko Sato,1,2 Pushker Kharecha,1,2 David Beerling,3 Valerie Masson-Delmotte,4 Mark Pagani,5 Maureen Raymo,6 Dana L. Royer,7 James C. Zachos8, Columbia University, 2008)

**If Americans do not act clearly and uncompromisingly, President Obama's successor will be offering another pleasant sounding energy plan with no substance.**

**America cannot continue floundering without a realistic energy policy.**

# PRESIDENT GEORGE W. BUSH'S ENERGY PLAN

**Today, President Bush Signed Into Law The First National Energy Plan In More Than A Decade.** The President's national energy plan will encourage energy efficiency and conservation, promote alternative and renewable energy sources, reduce our dependence on foreign sources of energy, increase domestic production, modernize the electricity grid, and encourage the expansion of nuclear energy.

**Background: The Energy Bill Promotes Investments in Energy Conservation and Efficiency**

**Energy Legislation Encourages Energy Conservation And Efficiency.** By supporting new energy efficient technologies, the government can offer every American better energy security at lower costs. More money is being spent on energy efficiency research today than ever before.

- **Promoting Residential Efficiency.** Technology offers the possibility of a "zero-energy" home. The average American home loses between 10 and 50 percent of its energy through inadequate insulation and inefficient lights and appliances. President Bush is committed to supporting research that promotes advances in energy efficiency, and the energy bill offers consumers tax credits for making energy efficiency improvements in their homes.

- **Increasing the Efficiency Of Appliances And Commercial Products.** The energy bill sets new minimum energy efficiency standards for a range of consumer and commercial products, including heaters, refrigerators, and lighting units. It also encourages the sale and production of energy efficient products, which increases the supply of available energy, helping families meet their bottom lines. Tax credits are available for highly efficient central air conditioners, heat pumps, and water heaters, as well as to upgrade thermostats, install exterior windows, and stop energy waste.

- **Reducing Federal Government Energy Usage.** The Federal government is the largest user of energy, and the energy bill calls on Federal agencies to lead by example and improve their energy efficiency. The energy bill reauthorizes the Energy Savings Performance Contract program, which allows private contractors to help Federal agencies improve the energy efficiency of their facilities. The bill also sets aggressive new goals for Federal energy efficiency and requires agencies to purchase Energy Star products.

- **Modernizing Domestic Energy Infrastructure.** The energy bill will help modernize our aging energy infrastructure to help reduce the risk of large-scale blackouts and minimize transmission bottlenecks. This will be accomplished by repealing outdated rules that discourage investment in new infrastructure, offering tax incentives for new transmission construction, and by encouraging the development of new technologies, such as superconducting power lines, to make the grid more efficient.

- **Diversifying the Nation's Energy Supply with Renewable Sources.** The energy bill will promote the use of renewable energy sources with tax credits for wind, solar, and biomass energy, including the first-ever tax credit for residential solar energy systems. The bill also expands research into developing hydrogen technologies and establishes a flexible, national Renewable Fuels Standard to encourage greater use of renewable fuels like ethanol and biodiesel.

- **Supporting A New Generation Of Energy-Efficient Vehicles.** In his FY 2006 Budget, President Bush called for new consumer tax credits for energy-efficient hybrid, clean-diesel, and fuel-cell vehicles. The energy bill will provide up to $3,400 per vehicle in tax credits to consumers for purchase of these cars, based on their fuel savings potential. Some of these cars can travel twice as far as conventional vehicles on one gallon of fuel, reducing U.S. dependence on foreign energy sources while producing lower emissions.

# PRESIDENT BARRACK OBAMA'S ENERGY PLAN

- **Develop and secure America's energy supplies:** We need to deploy American assets, innovation, and technology so that we can safely and responsibly develop more energy here at home and be a leader in the global energy economy. To get there, we need to:

    ◦ Expand Safe and Responsible Domestic Oil and Gas Development and Production (Based on President Obama's fossil fuel record, what are the chances for this happening?)

    ◦ Lead the World toward Safer and More Secure Energy Supplies (America's leadership in the world is severely limited at best.)

- **Provide consumers with choices to reduce costs and save energy:** Volatile gasoline prices reinforce the need for innovation that will make it easier and more affordable for consumers to buy more advanced and fuel-efficient vehicles, use alternative means of transportation, weatherize their homes and workplaces, and in doing so, save money and protect the environment. These measures help families' pocketbooks, reduce our dependence on finite energy sources and help create good jobs here in the United States. So, we're implementing policies that:

    ◦ Reduce Consumers Costs at the Pump with More Efficient Cars and Trucks (What about Americans that cannot afford new, more expensive vehicles?)

    ◦ Cut Energy Bills with More Efficient Homes and Buildings (Again, what about Americans that cannot afford the upgrades?)

- **Innovate our way to a clean energy future:** Leading the world in clean energy is critical to strengthening the American economy and winning the future. We can get there by creating markets for innovative clean technologies that are ready to deploy, and by funding cutting-edge research to produce the next generation of technologies. And as new, better, and more efficient technologies hit the market, the Federal government needs to put words into action and lead by example. That's why we need to:

    o Harness America's Clean Energy Potential so that 80 percent of electricity will come from clean energy sources by 2035 (Where and how did the 80% number originate?)

    o Win the future through Clean Energy Research and Development (Win what future?)

    o Lead by Example so that the Federal Government models best practices and clean energy technologies (Increased taxes to cover additional expenses.)

# OIL PRICE AND SELECTED GLOBAL MARKET EVENTS

The chart on the following page, obtained from the U.S. EIA, clearly identifies world events and their impact on oil prices. An important part of the chart is the clear upward trend in oil prices increasing from the low $20 per barrel price in 2000 to more than $100 per barrel in 2012. In other words, oil prices have more than quadrupled in approximately 12 years! If America does not develop all its fossil fuel resources, America's way of life is history.

## OIL PRICE AND SELECTED GLOBAL MARKET EVENTS

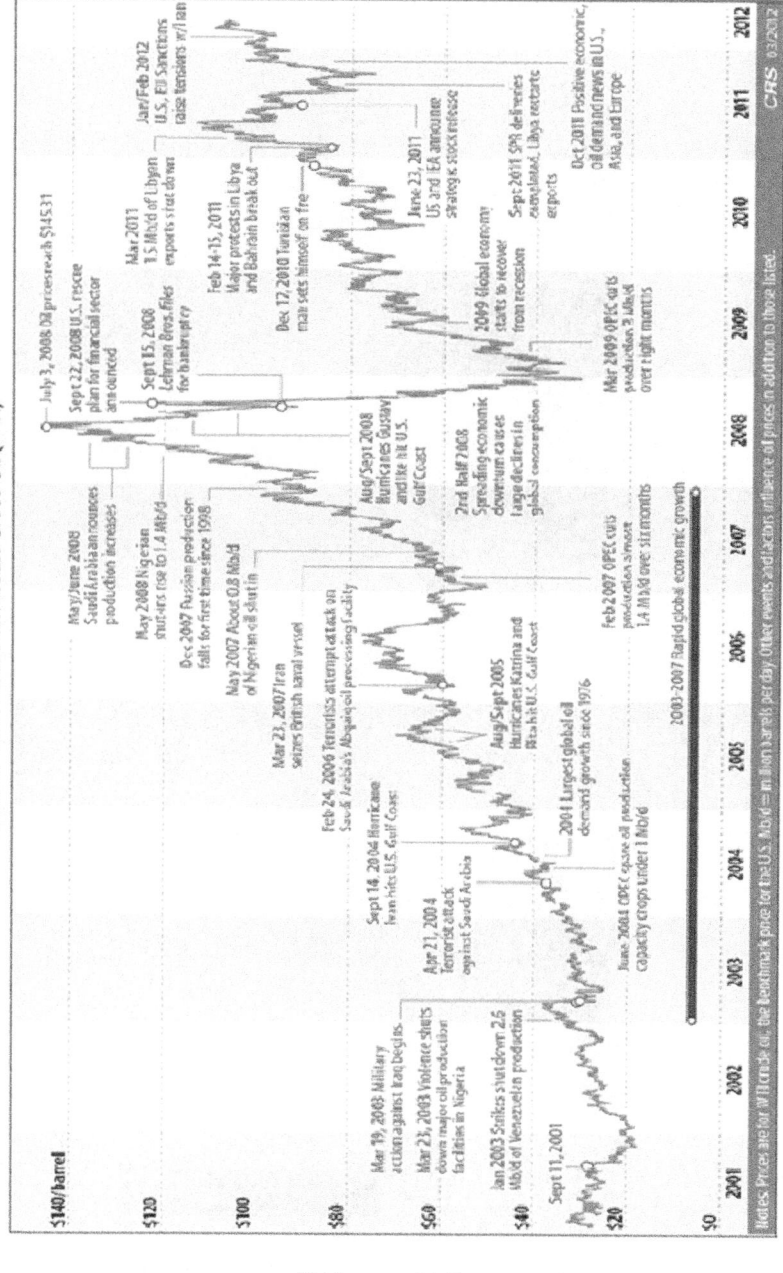

(Reference: 31.1)

**SECURE OUR SHIP! FUEL AMERICA NOW!**

## World Oil Reserves

(Reference: 32.1)

# THE CHALLENGE

The following is an excerpt from President Kennedy's speech at Rice University on September 12, 1962. (The complete speech is included in the next section of this book.)

### Every American needs to read the entire speech!

"But if I were to say, my fellow citizens, that we shall send to the moon, 240,000 miles away from the control station in Houston, a giant rocket more than 300 feet tall, the length of this football field, made of new metal alloys, some of which have not yet been invented, capable of standing heat and stresses several times more than have ever been experienced, fitted together with a precision better than the finest watch, carrying all the equipment needed for propulsion, guidance, control, communications, food and survival, on an untried mission, to an unknown celestial body, and then return it safely to earth, re-entering the atmosphere at speeds of over 25,000 miles per hour, causing heat about half that of the temperature of the sun--almost as hot as it is here today--**and do all this, and do it right, and do it first before this decade is out--then we must be bold.**"

(Reference: 33.1)

President Kennedy's speech is an example of the type of leadership an American President should possess. Other than Ronald Reagan, I challenge anyone to name a President of the United States since President Kennedy was assassinated, who has demonstrated similar leadership skills and responsibility. Isn't it time for Americans to elect a President that will confront America's problems straight on? The responsibility for America having had only 2 Presidents with the leadership skills plus the sense of responsibility demonstrated by Presidents Kennedy and Reagan must be borne by America's voters. (Another good example of Presidential leadership is contained in President Reagan's *'Tear Down This Wall'* speech.)

Fact 1: Global warming and climate change are occurring and appear to be the result of an increased level of atmospheric CO2. Fact 2: The earth's atmosphere contains more than enough CO2 to create an environment completely inhospitable for humans. Fact 3: Without human intervention, it could take nature literally thousands of years to reduce the current level of atmospheric CO2. Fact 4: No amount of reduction in carbon emissions resulting from the consumption of fossil fuels will eliminate global warming. Fact 5: There is no substitute for oil; not today or in the foreseeable future. Fact 6: As oil prices have escalated, America's economy, as well as most of the economies of the world, has deteriorated to the point that the future of many Americans is grim at best.

**It should be obvious the energy path America's leaders have selected, is going to lead to additional hardships and sacrifices for most Americans. This might be acceptable if the light at the end of the tunnel was not an oncoming train. The final fact is: America is going to have to create a robust economy to combat global warming which will require the development of all of America's fossil fuel resources. Anything less than an all-out commitment to create the world's strongest economy will only lead to economic and environmental disaster. As American voters, it is up to us to change the course of mankind! As American voters we must elect leaders based on proven leadership skills.**

Try to imagine if America had a President in the class of Kennedy and Reagan. What if that person got in front of Americans and presented an energy plan similar to the Fuel America Now energy plan? America's low cost energy would return manufacturers to America. In short order, America's economy would regain its vitality and create jobs for Americans as well as create opportunity for entrepreneurs. America would be on the path to end global warming.

# THE CHALLENGE

In all probability, the world leaders would publicly oppose America's efforts. Privately, the leaders of the world will know that if mankind is to get off the path to extermination, it will be due to Americans assuming the responsibility for eliminating global warming as well as possessing the confidence and courage necessary to confront global warming head on.

Reducing $CO_2$ emissions, ('Plan A'), may make good press and make Americans feel better but the fact remains that unless the current levels of atmospheric $CO_2$ is reduced, global warming will continue unimpeded. Reducing America's or even the world's current and future $CO_2$ emissions from the use of fossil fuels will not stop the continued buildup of atmospheric $CO_2$. Even if fossil fuels were entirely eliminated, which is not possible, there will be significantly more $CO_2$ emitted into the atmosphere than returns to earth.

Picture President Obama or his successor making the following commitment and the impact it would have on the American economy.

*"Fellow Americans, thank you for permitting me the time to speak with you. Without a doubt, this is the most important speech I have ever made and most likely will be the most important speech I will ever give.*

*America, as well as the rest of the world, must prepare for climate change which is primarily the result of modern human activity. There is nothing Americans can do to avoid the impending climate change. But, Americans can reduce the impact and duration of climate change! Unfortunately, the actions required to protect Americans as well as all mankind, will not be supported by most other countries. Regardless of the support or lack of support from other countries, the fact remains that without aggressive action by America, the lives of Americans and mankind will be radically altered, if not totally eliminated, in a relatively short period of time.*

## SECURE OUR SHIP! FUEL AMERICA NOW!

*As President of the United States, my responsibility is to authorize actions and legislation that protects and enhances the lives of Americans. America remains as the strongest, most envied country in the world due to its Capitalistic economy. Americans have thrived on opportunities other countries do not offer. My actions will revitalize America's economy providing opportunities for all Americans. The actions required to revive America's economic system will likely receive ridicule from the political extremes of both parties. The public media will likely attack my actions and proposed legislation.*

*Fellow Americans, I intend to do my best to make sure you are informed as to what is being proposed, why it is being proposed, the potential risks as well as the expected rewards. It will be up to you to make the final decision and let your representatives know how you expect them to vote. The future of America, as well as mankind is in our hands.*

*The actions America must take to protect Americans and mankind will likely result in the other countries of the world accusing America of adopting a policy of isolationism. Nothing can be further from the truth. Yes, America must protect its way of life but America's way of life cannot be sustained without aggressively confronting the environmental damage of the past and minimizing the environmental damage of the future. The fact is, due to cultural differences, life styles and expectancies throughout the World; there is no way a consensus can be arrived at that will prepare mankind for the impending climate change as well as the actions required to return earth to the point it is more supportive of human life. It's just not going to happen. America must assume the responsibility to use its abundant energy resources and capitalistic economy to conquer climate change. If other countries want to participate with America or even compete with America in overcoming climate change, America welcomes their involvement.*

*The consumption of fossil fuels is acknowledged as the foremost contributor to the increasing level of atmospheric $CO_2$, which is considered the direct cause of climate change. Unfortunately, human life as we know it cannot exist without fossil fuels, specifically oil. Furthermore, reducing the consumption of fossil fuels will reduce $CO_2$ emissions and at best minimally defer the ultimate impact of climate change. The fact is that due to the current and increasing needs of a growing world population, $CO_2$ emissions into the atmosphere will not only continue to exceed $CO_2$ naturally returning to earth; the*

## THE CHALLENGE

*differential will increase significantly as world population continues to expand. Baring a catastrophic reduction in world population, efforts to stop climate change by relying solely on reduced consumption of fossil fuels are futile.*

*America maintains a unique position in today's world. America's capitalistic economy is second to no other country. America's deep-seated attitude of individualism and self-reliance based on a 'can do' philosophy is not duplicated in any other society. Add to this America's access to virtually unlimited energy resources, and you realize only America is capable of taking the actions required to manage climate change. Also, unless America acts quickly and decisively, the future of America, as well as mankind, is bleak at best. The real question becomes: What must Americans do to save America as well as all mankind?*

*America must take whatever action required to develop and sustain a strong and growing economy. America must develop and implement the technology which will allow America to not only survive climate change but to prosper. America must prosper at the level required to fund the development and implementation of the technology required to monitor and control greenhouse gases, including atmospheric $CO_2$. The creation of such an economy will require secure, stable and affordable energy. America must become energy independent within 5 years or less.*

*If America is to rapidly become energy independent, the following actions must be taken. Actions that can be accomplished by Presidential directive will be made immediately. Actions requiring Congressional approval will be submitted immediately. The first regulation is to restrict the purchase of fossil fuels, as well as products produced from fossil fuels, to be purchased only by individuals, companies and organizations that refine, market, distribute and/or use the products in the production of new products. From this time forward, it is illegal to speculate or purchase fossil fuels or products derived from fossil fuels, as an investment.*

*All properties owned or controlled by the Federal Government with known fossil fuel resources will be regularly auctioned to qualified developers. Any land auctioned for the development of fossil fuel resources must be promptly developed or the lease will be forfeited. All government properties that have not been explored for the development of energy resources will be assessed. All development on federal government properties will be conducted in a manner that minimizes environmental damages. Energy produced from government controlled properties will be subject to pricing established by the government.*

*Legal actions undertaken to slow down or even stop the development of Federal lands can only be filed in Federal Courts. In the event the plaintiff losses the legal action, the Plaintiff will be responsible for the defendant's legal costs, as well as any financial losses by the defendant associated with the legal filing. The purpose of this action is the elimination of frivolous legal suits as well as local court actions that may occur due to local prejudices, not legal justification."*

### ... The speech will continue with additional components of the FAN energy plan. ...

**A variation of the speech will be made at some point in the future**; the sooner the better! America will return to its roots of promoting individual independence and self sufficiency. Additionally, the President will quickly establish himself as the leader America, as well as the leader the world. The fact remains, until America returns to its roots of aggressive economic actions and generates the funds required for developing technologies and methods required to monitor and control global warming, America as well as the world will continue on the path of human destruction.

As an American, do you agree, disagree or just don't like the ideas and conclusions presented in this book? If you agree with the position this book presents, are you prepared to get involved in the efforts to change America's energy, economic and environmental policy? If you disagree with this book, are you prepared to justify the reasoning for your objections? If you just don't like what this book presents, you need to think about the reasons why this book offends you.

**If you support how the Fuel America Now, (FAN), energy plan tackles America's energy, economic and environmental policies, please**

let your friends know about this book. Also, bring FAN to the attention of your elected leaders and let them know that your vote will be based on their support for FAN. Also, let them know that you are making sure your friends and associates are aware of the FAN energy policy.

If you disagree with any idea or conclusion contained in this book and can substantiate the reason(s) for your disagreement along with how you would meet America's energy requirements to improve our economy and environment; please forward your comments and supporting documentation to: SOSFAN@BizzEB.com. Your input will be reviewed and in the event a fact, idea or conclusion presented by this book is erroneous, the appropriate corrective action will be taken. **As Americans, we must work together to make sure our government leads America in a direction that is in the best interest of most Americans.**

If you just don't like the ideas, conclusions or other material contained in this book don't bury your head in the sand. **Americans as well as entire human race are on a path which will end life as we know it; unless America makes major efforts and investments in the technology required to monitor and control atmospheric $CO_2$. This is a fact that cannot be ignored.**

   Final Thoughts from America's First and Greatest President!

**In President George Washington's farewell address he urges the people to place their identity as Americans above their identities as members of a state, city, or region, and focus their efforts and affection on the country above all other local interests. President Washington further asks the people to look beyond any slight differences between them in religion, manners, habits, and political principles, and place their independence and liberty above all else.**

**Washington warns the people that political factions who seek to obstruct the execution of the laws created by the government, or prevent the constitutional branches from enacting the powers provided them by the constitution may claim to be working in the interest of (and) answering popular demands or solving pressing problems, but their true intentions are to take the power from the people and place it in the hands of unjust men.**

## Background on President Washington

*When America won its independence, George Washington was Commander and Chief of America's armed forces. Washington could have easily seized power and declared himself 'King of America'. As a matter of fact there were influential individuals urging Washington to assume the position of King. Washington refused and was later elected as America's President. President Washington was prepared to step down after his first term but was persuaded to run for a second term due to the fact that America was not ready for him to leave office. President Washington used his second term to prepare Americans for the next President. In his second term, President Washington put in place many procedures which are still followed. More importantly, President Washington understood the fact that if America was to remain independent plus Americans were to continue to enjoy liberty; personal and political differences must be secondary when enacting policies, laws and actions.*

**Unfortunately, Americans have lost sight of what it is to be an American rather than a Democrat or Republican and/or a Conservative or Liberal. If America is to continue to exist, Americans must regain control of elected leaders and make sure they perform their jobs in a manner which is in the best interest most Americans. Remember elected leaders including America's President, work for you and me. As Americans, we have the final say in who we hire, (elect), as well as who needs to be fired!**

# JOHN F. KENNEDY MOON SPEECH – RICE UNIVERSITY

September 12, 1962

President Pitzer, Mr. Vice President, Governor, Congressman Thomas, Senator Wiley, and Congressman Miller, Mr. Webb, Mr. Bell, scientists, distinguished guests, and ladies and gentlemen:

I appreciate your president having made me an honorary visiting professor, and I will assure you that my first lecture will be very brief.

I am delighted to be here, and I'm particularly delighted to be here on this occasion.

We meet at a college noted for knowledge, in a city noted for progress, in a State noted for strength, and we stand in need of all three, for we meet in an hour of change and challenge, in a decade of hope and fear, in an age of both knowledge and ignorance. The greater our knowledge increases, the greater our ignorance unfolds.

Despite the striking fact that most of the scientists that the world has ever known are alive and working today, despite the fact that this Nation's own scientific manpower is doubling every 12 years in a rate of growth more than three times that of our population as a whole, despite that, the vast stretches of the unknown and the unanswered and the unfinished still far outstrip our collective comprehension.

No man can fully grasp how far and how fast we have come, but condense, if you will, the 50,000 years of man's recorded history in a time span of but a half-century. Stated in these terms, we know very little about the first 40 years, except at the end of them advanced man had learned to use the skins of animals to cover them. Then about 10 years ago, under this standard, man emerged from his caves to construct other kinds of shelter. Only five years ago man learned to write and use a cart with wheels. Christianity began less than two years ago. The printing press came this year, and then less than two months ago, during this whole 50-year span of human history, the steam engine provided a new source of power.

Newton explored the meaning of gravity. Last month electric lights and telephones and automobiles and airplanes became available. Only last week did we develop penicillin and television and nuclear power, and now if America's new spacecraft succeeds in reaching Venus, we will have literally reached the stars before midnight tonight.

This is a breathtaking pace, and such a pace cannot help but create new ills as it dispels old, new ignorance, new problems, new dangers. Surely the opening vistas of space promise high costs and hardships, as well as high reward.

So it is not surprising that some would have us stay where we are a little longer to rest, to wait. But this city of Houston, this State of Texas, this country of the United States was not built by those who waited and rested and wished to look behind them. This country was conquered by those who moved forward--and so will space.

William Bradford, speaking in 1630 of the founding of the Plymouth Bay Colony, said that all great and honorable actions are accompanied with great difficulties, and both must be enterprised and overcome with answerable courage.

If this capsule history of our progress teaches us anything, it is that man, in his quest for knowledge and progress, is determined and cannot be deterred. The exploration of space will go ahead, whether we join in it or not, and it is one of the great adventures of all time, and no nation which expects to be the leader of other nations can expect to stay behind in the race for space.

Those who came before us made certain that this country rode the first waves of the industrial revolutions, the first waves of modern invention, and the first wave of nuclear power, and this generation does not intend to founder in the backwash of the coming age of space. We mean to be a part of it--we mean to lead it. For the eyes of the world now look into space, to the moon and to the planets beyond, and we have vowed that we shall not see it governed by a hostile flag of conquest, but by a banner of freedom and peace. We have vowed that we shall not see space filled with weapons of mass destruction, but with instruments of knowledge and understanding.

Yet the vows of this Nation can only be fulfilled if we in this Nation are first, and, therefore, we intend to be first. In short, our leadership in science and in industry, our hopes for peace and security, our obligations to ourselves as well as others, all require us to make this effort, to solve these mysteries, to solve them for the good of all men, and to become the world's leading space-faring nation.

We set sail on this new sea because there is new knowledge to be gained, and new rights to be won, and they must be won and used for the progress of all people. For space science, like nuclear science and all technology, has no conscience of its own. Whether it will become a force for good or ill depends on man, and only if the United States occupies a position of pre-eminence can we help decide whether this new ocean will be a sea of peace or a new terrifying theater of war. I do not say the we should or will go unprotected against the hostile misuse of space any more than we go unprotected against the hostile use of land or sea, but I do say that space can be explored and mastered without feeding the fires of war, without repeating the mistakes that man has made in extending his writ around this globe of ours.

There is no strife, no prejudice, no national conflict in outer space as yet. Its hazards are hostile to us all. Its conquest deserves the best of all mankind, and its opportunity for peaceful cooperation many never come again. But why, some say, the moon? Why choose this as our goal? And they may well ask why climb the highest mountain? Why, 35 years ago, fly the Atlantic? Why does Rice play Texas?

We choose to go to the moon. We choose to go to the moon in this decade and do the other things, not because they are easy, but because they are hard, because that goal will serve to organize and measure the best of our energies and skills, because that challenge is one that we are willing to accept, one we are unwilling to postpone, and one which we intend to win, and the others, too.

It is for these reasons that I regard the decision last year to shift our efforts in space from low to high gear as among the most important decisions that will be made during my incumbency in the office of the Presidency.

In the last 24 hours we have seen facilities now being created for the greatest and most complex exploration in man's history. We have felt the ground shake and the air shattered by the testing of a Saturn C-1 booster rocket, many times as powerful as the Atlas which launched John Glenn, generating power equivalent to 10,000 automobiles with their accelerators on the floor. We have seen the site where the F-1 rocket engines, each one as powerful as all eight engines of the Saturn combined, will be clustered together to make the advanced Saturn missile, assembled in a new building to be built at Cape Canaveral as tall as a 48 story structure, as wide as a city block, and as long as two lengths of this field.

Within these last 19 months at least 45 satellites have circled the earth. Some 40 of them were "made in the United States of America" and they were far more sophisticated and supplied far more knowledge to the people of the world than those of the Soviet Union.

The Mariner spacecraft now on its way to Venus is the most intricate instrument in the history of space science. The accuracy of that shot is comparable to firing a missile from Cape Canaveral and dropping it in this stadium between the 40-yard lines.

Transit satellites are helping our ships at sea to steer a safer course. Tiros 'weather' satellites have given us unprecedented warnings of hurricanes and storms, and will do the same for forest fires and icebergs.

We have had our failures, but so have others, even if they do not admit them. And they may be less public.

To be sure, we are behind, and will be behind for some time in manned flight. But we do not intend to stay behind, and in this decade, we shall make up and move ahead.

The growth of our science and education will be enriched by new knowledge of our universe and environment, by new techniques of learning and mapping and observation, by new tools and computers for industry, medicine, the home as well as the school. Technical institutions, such as Rice, will reap the harvest of these gains.

And finally, the space effort itself, while still in its infancy, has already created a great number of new companies, and tens of thousands of new jobs. Space and related industries are generating new demands in investment and skilled personnel, and this city and this State, and this region, will share greatly in this growth. What was once the furthest outpost on the old frontier of the West will be the furthest outpost on the new frontier of science and space. Houston, your City of Houston, with its Manned Spacecraft Center, will become the heart of a large scientific and engineering community. During the next 5 years the National Aeronautics and Space Administration expects to double the number of scientists and engineers in this area, to increase its outlays for salaries and expenses to $60 million a year; to invest some $200 million in plant and laboratory facilities; and to direct or contract for new space efforts over $1 billion from this Center in this City.

To be sure, all this costs us all a good deal of money. This year's space budget is three times what it was in January 1961, and it is greater than the space budget of the previous eight years combined. That budget now stands at $5,400 million a year--a staggering sum, though somewhat less than we pay for cigarettes and cigars every year. Space expenditures will soon rise some more, from 40 cents per person per week to more than 50 cents a week for every man, woman and child in the United Stated, for we have given this program a high national priority--even though I realize that this is in some measure an act of faith and vision, for we do not now know what benefits await us.

But if I were to say, my fellow citizens, that we shall send to the moon, 240,000 miles away from the control station in Houston, a giant rocket more than 300 feet tall, the length of this football field, made of new metal alloys, some of which have not yet been invented, capable of standing heat and stresses several times more than have ever been experienced, fitted together with a precision better than the finest watch, carrying all the equipment needed for propulsion, guidance, control, communications, food and survival, on an untried mission, to an unknown celestial body, and then return it safely to earth, re-entering the atmosphere at speeds of over 25,000 miles per hour, causing heat about half that of the temperature of the sun--almost as hot as it is here today--and do all this, and do it right, and do it first before this decade is out--then we must be bold.

I'm the one who is doing all the work, so we just want you to stay cool for a minute. [laughter]

However, I think we're going to do it, and I think that we must pay what needs to be paid. I don't think we ought to waste any money, but I think we ought to do the job. And this will be done in the decade of the sixties. It may be done while some of you are still here at school at this college and university. It will be done during the term of office of some of the people who sit here on this platform. But it will be done. And it will be done before the end of this decade.

I am delighted that this university is playing a part in putting a man on the moon as part of a great national effort of the United States of America.

Many years ago the great British explorer George Mallory, who was to die on Mount Everest, was asked why did he want to climb it. He said, "Because it is there."

Well, space is there, and we're going to climb it, and the moon and the planets are there, and new hopes for knowledge and peace are there. And, therefore, as we set sail we ask God's blessing on the most hazardous and dangerous and greatest adventure on which man has ever embarked.

Thank you.

# REFERENCE

The graphics, tables and pictures presented in this book are in the **public domain** in the United States because it is a work prepared by an officer or employee of the United States Government as part of that person's official duties under the terms of Title 17, Chapter 1, Section 105 of the US Code. The graphics, tables and pictures presented in this book were obtained from:

EPA – Environmental Protection Agency
EIA – Energy Information Agency
NOAA – National Oceanic and Atmospheric Association
NASA – National Aeronautics and Space Administration
CIA – Central Intelligence Agency
DOE – Department of Energy
NREL – DOE's National Renewable Energy Laboratory (This is a valuable resource to locate information on America's renewable energy research: http://www.nrel.gov/)

**The Internet links to the graphics used in this book were obtained as stated below:**

<u>Reference</u>     <u>Link – Source</u>

2.1 Created by author.
2.2 http://earthobservatory.nasa.gov/GlobalMaps/?eocn=topnav&eoci=globalmaps
2.32 http://heartland.org/sites/default/files/NIPCC%20Final.pdf
4.1 http://www.infoplease.com/ipa/A0883352.html
5.1 http://www.esrl.noaa.gov/gmd/outreach/behind_the_scenes/gases.html
5.2 http://www.eia.gov/tools/faqs/faq.cfm?id=73&t=11
7.1 http://www.epa.gov/climatestudents/documents/temp-and-co2.pdf

7.2 http://news.yahoo.com/whats-number-carbon-dioxide-level-unseen-human-history-005622242--abc-news-tech.html
7.3 http://www.esrl.noaa.gov/gmd/aggi/
7.4 http://www.noaanews.noaa.gov/stories2012/20120801_esrlcarbonstudy.html
8.1 http://www.epa.gov/climatechange/ghgemissions/gases/co2.html
8.2 http://research.noaa.gov/News/NewsArchive/LatestNews/TabId/684/ArtMID/1768/ArticleID/10216/Greenhouse-gases-continue-climbing-2012-a-record-year.aspx
9.1 http://www.eia.gov/totalenergy/data/annual/pecss_diagram.cfm
10.1 http://www.nacsonline.com/News/NACSDaily/Pages/default.aspx
10.2 http://www.nacsonline.com/News/NACSDaily/Pages/default.aspx
10.3 http://www.eia.gov/forecasts/steo/special/pdf/2013_sp_05.pdf
11.1 http://www.eia.gov/kids/energy.cfm?page=oil_home-basics
11.2 https://www.pbs.org/independentlens/classroom/wwo/petroleum.pdf
13.1 http://commons.wikimedia.org/wiki/File:Gusher_Okemah_OK_1922.jpg
15.2 Created by author.
15.3 http://en.wikipedia.org/wiki/File:Alberta_Taciuk_Processor.PNG

15.4 Created by author.
16.1 http://www.eia.gov/todayinenergy/detail.cfm?id=4390
19.1 http://www.epa.gov/climatestudents/solutions/technologies/nuclear.html
20.1 http://www.epa.gov/ncea/biofuels/
21.1 http://www.usbr.gov/uc/power/hydropwr/genbasics.html
22.1 http://geo-energy.org/reports/environmental%20guide.pdf
23.1 http://www.eia.gov/energyexplained/index.cfm?page=solar_environment
24.1 http://www.eia.gov/kids/energy.cfm?page=wind_home-basics
25.1 http://www.eia.gov/kids/energy.cfm?page=biomass_home-basics
26.1 Created from government agency tables by the book's author.

# REFERENCE

**In the event additional energy and environmental is needed, follow the links listed above.**

Unless otherwise indicated, most of the information contained in this book was obtained from and/or verified on web sites operated by the above mentioned U. S. government agencies.

**IPCC 2013 Report on Climate Change web site link: http://www.ipcc.ch/report/ar5/wg1/**

Made in the USA
Coppell, TX
21 March 2022